Soul Custody

Sparing Children from Divorce

By Pamela Henry

Soul Custody Press
Redlands, California

Copyright © 2025 Pamela L. Henry Living Trust

All rights reserved. Printed in the United States of America. No part of this publication may be reproduced, distributed or transmitted in any form or by any means, including photocopying, recording, or other electronic or mechanical methods, without the prior written permission of the publisher, except in the case of brief quotations embodied in critical reviews and certain other noncommercial uses permitted by copyright law. Requests: soulcustody.pamela@gmail.com.

Unless otherwise indicated, all Scripture quotations are taken from the Holy Bible, New Living Translation® (NLT®). Copyright © 1996, 2004, 2015 by Tyndale House Foundation. Used by permission of Tyndale House Publishers, Carol Stream, Illinois 60188. All rights reserved worldwide. The "NLT" and "New Living Translation" are registered trademarks of Tyndale House Ministries.

Published by Soul Custody Press
Redlands, California

Book and Cover design by Kamaruddin Ahmad

Cover Image: 1976 oil portrait, Tijuana artist Juan Badía (1938-2020)

Printed in the United States of America

ISBN: 978-0-9907848-9-0

Library of Congress Control Number:
2025904979

Disclaimer

This book, author and publisher do not represent professional legal, psychological or spiritual advice. The opinions and interpretations expressed in this memoir are the author's alone and do not reflect the views of others mentioned or her opinions on any person's situation. In defining its intended audience as "weak cases for divorce," this book is not a determinant of which cases fit escapist vs. non-escapist. By reading this book, readers assume full responsibility for actions, decisions and emotions that result. Please prioritize self-care while reading this memoir. It contains references to emotionally disturbing material, including divorce trauma, childhood memories, sexual abuse, mental illness, and filicide. If you are in immediate danger, call 911. In the U.S. and Canada, the National Domestic Violence Hotline is 800-799-SAFE (7233). Parents and youth in crisis anywhere in the United States can call or text the confidential California Parent & Youth Helpline at 855-427-2736, operated by the non-profit Parents Anonymous.

Dedication

To parents at the crossroads of divorce:

May this book serve as a gentle intervention, offering a moment to reconsider. Before you make a decision that alters your family's future, pause to consider the long-term impact. Healing is possible, and your choice today can determine a better tomorrow for your family's future.

Acknowledgments

First and foremost, I give thanks to Jesus who blessed me with a good marriage and three beautiful daughters who along with their father have my sincere gratitude for their support of this memoir. Thank you to my mentors Shelly La Botte and JaDawn Bean, Pastor Josh Howeth, Stephanie Whiting, Samara Kopelman, Ruby Roetker, editor Valerie Jones, producer Jon Lobb, the Christian Writers Institute, the 540 Writers Community, All Caps Marketing Agency, Book Launchers, and C.S. Lewis & Co. Publicity. To everyone who reads this book: May our collective efforts spare many children from divorce.

Table of Contents

Preface 1
Introduction: Point of Return 5

Antidote #1 - Averting the Prevailing Sadness .. 18
    Visit a Divorce Support Group 23
    Staying for the Children is Wisdom 29
    Before You Would Tell the Children 32

Antidote #2 - Restoring God's Covenant in Marriage 40
    Doubts Can Strengthen Faith 45
    The Word on Marriage 55
    If God Hates Divorce, Shouldn't I? 56
    Seek Him First. 61
    Get Honest 67

Antidote #3 - Overcoming Anxiety Through Prayer and Faith 70
    The Pinball Machine 73
    Don't Add to your Child's ACE Score 78

Antidote #4 - Remembering the Benefits of Full-Time Parenting 83
    Consider the Family Life that You Risk Losing . 88
    Weighing Loss of Full-time Access 91

Antidote #5 - Healing from Old Wounds 94
    It Wasn't About Him 95
    Deeper Reasons 97
    Origins of Selfishness 101
    A Glimpse of Hope 108

Putting Children First 111
Your Children's Entire World Depends Upon You
Two. 116
A Word To Those Who Regret Divorce 119
A Final Word to Married Parents 122

Epilogue **126**
Appendix **128**
    Citations 128
    Quiz 130
    Study Guide 131

Preface

"Don't copy the behavior and customs of this world, but let God transform you into a new person by changing the way you think. Then you will learn to know God's will for you, which is good and pleasing and perfect."
~ Romans 12:2

When I read my daughter's journal three years after our divorce, I knew I'd made a mistake. Her entry: "I just miss Mom. I'm hating life because:

- My acne
- My friends when they're mean
- My parents being divorced
- My wardrobe
- My hair."

I never imagined that our divorce could make it to the Top 5 List of "Things I Hate About Life." And yet, there it was etched in the heart of a pre-teen – the loss that keeps losing, years after a marriage ends.

If you're a parent struggling with married life right now, pull up a chair for the message I want to impart. I'd been married for 16 years, now divorced for 17. I want to share some of the hard lessons I've learned. I'm here to talk about the regret that often comes with divorce and tell you what I wish someone had told me before I filed.

Without realizing it, I became part of what I call "Club Thirty," the 30% of those who end up regretting divorce.[1] This book is dedicated to intervention for parents before they become potential members.

My daughter's list inspired my antidotes for married parents: The Top 5 Regrets about divorce, not ranked but rather all taking turns in severity:

- The overwhelming sadness that descended upon my daughters, ages 1, 7, and 10.
- Dishonoring God and my husband, thinking I was honoring myself.
- The chronic anxiety that infiltrated their lives from the trauma of divorce.
- The irreversible splitting of their time between two homes; cutting in half not only their time with each parent but also my time with them, and their father's time with them, for the rest of our lives.
- Hurting my children by passing on the generational wound of divorce, a legacy I never intended to leave.

---

[1] *Club 30 is my name rounding off the percentage who regret divorce from Page 37 of a 2016 Relationship, Marriage and Divorce survey by Avvo.com.*

This book is written specifically for those in situations like mine; what I call "escapist divorces." These are divorces where there is no abuse, no addiction, no physical infidelity, no life-threatening issues, but just a desire to avoid facing something difficult. We are parents who don't realize we are trying to escape ourselves.

Marriages are like pressure cookers for spiritual growth. And when it's your turn to face issues, if you can't take the heat, the urge is to leave the marriage in order to avoid yourself. Divorce is so ugly, no one wants to look at it in the mirror. But my prayer as you read this is you will look deeper to see the beauty of your marriage through God's eyes and your children's hearts, and then perhaps decide to stay for those reasons.

The majority of divorces are not caused by life-threatening or safety issues such as abuse or addiction. More often, reasons given for divorce are infidelity, communication problems, financial issues, or lack of intimacy. In this book, I retrace my steps to find where I first went wrong. And now, with a different view of things, I look deeper like I should have done back then.

See if you can find yourself in my story as a child of divorce or as a parent on the way to divorce. By telling you everything I wish I'd been told, it's like getting to go back and do it right. It won't bring back *my* marriage, but it could save yours.

In "Point of Return," my story provides context for the rest of the book. Then, I address each of the five regrets, calling them antidotes.

Divorce is such a painful topic. So, for comfort, I've included Biblical Scripture and prayers on your behalf. It's decidedly Christian in that my personal relationship with God was the key ingredient missing from my understanding of marriage. Questions at the end of each chapter provide for reflection and discussion. They're repeated at the end of the book in a study guide that includes blank pages for your responses.

Ask yourself one initial question: Would you still divorce if you knew ahead of time that one day you'd regret it? Let's find out if you're a candidate for Club Thirty. If you are, let this book help you stay married.

Introduction: Point of Return

"You have heard the commandment that says, 'You must not commit adultery.' But I say, anyone who even looks at a woman with lust has already committed adultery with her in his heart."

~ **Matthew 5:27-28**

Divorce is a legacy, and it is passed on like an inheritance. I can only trace it back to my maternal grandparents. What was scandalous for my grandmother was only socially frowned upon for my mother by the 1970s. But by the time it got to me in the 2000s, the action of divorcing became championed and contagious.

When I got engaged in 1990, I felt at higher risk for it because of my parents divorcing when I was 7. So, I did a lot of work in premarital counseling to help heal the past and not repeat it. This enabled me to face marriage with confidence, and we got off to a great start.

My journals tell the story of a strong marriage for 15 years—after two years of dating and two more engaged. By our sixth wedding anniversary, we had our first daughter. We had one miscarriage. Our rainbow daughter came along a year later.[2] And our third daughter was the

---

[2] A "rainbow" child is a term used for the child born after one was lost.

answer to my 40th birthday wish. Together, we created a beautiful family.

It's the nature of divorce to render irrelevant the love story of the relationship, once punctuated by its ending. So, I'll skip the glory days in favor of the question people ask: "If it was so good, why did it end?" My response at the time was to neutralize blame with, "We grew apart."

But this was me avoiding responsibility and accountability. The real answers were only revealed to me years after the divorce, through prayer.

From today's perspective, it looks like my decline began in the 13th year of marriage, when our two girls were 7 and 4. The eldest, reaching the age of my own parents' divorce, was a missed red flag. Then, while away at a conference of a 12-step program called Adult Children of Alcoholics, I recovered the full memory of an incestuous incident by my father. I'd already spent my adult life dealing with this and other childhood issues in therapy. But my response to it this time was different. My initial wrong turn in the heart occurred when, soon after the revelation, I started developing one-way obsessions over men who were not my husband. These mental preoccupations confined to my diaries began slowly eroding my commitment to marriage without my understanding their gravity, more like "Adultery in the heart." These men did not even know of my affection, so it felt safe and non-threatening. Incest may have prompted relationship obsession as a way to escape, but I see those one-way secret emotional affairs as the real rift-causer, like any other addiction. I didn't know yet about the Scripture naming adultery in the heart, but I was living it firsthand. Two years later, my marriage ended for the same reason.

It took a year of therapy before I could confront my father with kindness, honesty, and forgiveness. You'd think me forgiving my father would help heal my marriage, but I was still emotionally cheating. And then, my father disowned me; he cut off all contact after I confronted him. I didn't account for the impact of this. Instead of facing this new rejection, I paid it forward to my husband: rejecting him and the marriage. Unconscious at the time, this "pay it forward" method of avoiding pain passes on the rejection to someone else as fast as possible. Think of incest as broken trust, then re-enacting that by breaking trust in your adult intimate life. I was, in fact, repeating my own dreaded history, joining the real-life statistics on how childhood abuses ruin intimate relationships later in life.

Lesson learned: *Don't make your spouse (and as a result, your children) pay for your parents' behaviors.*

At the time, I had no religious foundation that could make a difference, even though I had a prayer life and attended church by myself. I was not "a believer." Though identifying as Christian, I didn't turn to the Lord to repent from my ways or find strength for the marriage to endure. My husband had withdrawn from Christianity long before we even met and became agnostic by the time we divorced. And even though my husband and I were in some serious professional marital counseling as we neared the end of our marriage, these emotional affairs – still one-way – were undermining all chances of success. I was on a fast track to outrun the demons from my past.

So, our marriage didn't survive this particular hurdle, though it had hurled over many other obstacles before. I had no grace or forgiveness for myself, and felt I had to leave the marriage to stand my own guilt of wanting to further pursue those one-way affairs. Even when things eventually came out in therapy, before the divorce, my husband offered me plenty of grace and forgiveness. He was willing to move on and forgive the transgressions, but I insisted on leaving. It was pride: "Don't want to cheat on him, so better to leave him?" I didn't know that, according to the Bible, I had already committed adultery. I also didn't understand yet that nothing would be more cruel than divorcing.

The rueful day I filed for divorce was April 4, 2008. It became final on October 9 that year. The girls were only 1, 7, and 10. It was the fastest and the nicest divorce I'd ever heard of, like "Best Divorce Ever," which is a sad trophy to have on your shelf. We never saw a courtroom then. We used one lawyer to knock out a marital settlement agreement. We had equal, shared legal and physical custody of the children. We made it like Daddy was getting an additional home for our girls. This is the facade that fools you into thinking, "The kids are fine." Under the best of circumstances, divorce is still traumatic.

The fact we had an ideal custody arrangement and got along well showed me the pure impact of divorce under the best of circumstances: no need for courtrooms, 50/50 joint physical and legal custody, living nearby, and actively co-parenting daily. So mine isn't a divorce regret because of conflict. I was determined to do it well and not fight over money like my parents. No, this ambitious agenda worked against me in this way: having failed my mission to not repeat the family divorce legacy, pride vowed to make it the best co-parenting job on the planet. This pride, coming from a deep sense of failure, paved the way for all kinds of missed cues to really recognize what our three children needed from me – my undivided attention.

Once I was out of the marriage, the affairs lost their purpose. There was no need for their numbing effect anymore, because divorce itself puts you in a state of shock sufficient to block out past, present, and future. The deep sense of marital failure caused me to look for the nearest replacement. A 5-week rebounding relationship after divorce (not one of the original three obsessions) had a bombshell effect on my children. I'll never forget the puzzled look of my 7-year-old girl looking at my overnight engagement ring: "Mom, you've only known him for 3 weeks!" Even she knew better at her age.

That reality check kept me focused on motherhood for five straight years without a date as the effects of divorce fueled a food addiction only salvation by Jesus Christ could cure.[3] Like all addictions, eating disorders are just symptomatic of the need for God. In those five years, I wrote a book about it called *The Resting Place, A Graveside Diary,* coining a new term, Post-Divorce Destruction Disorder. Bottom line:

---

[3] Food addiction recovery can be found at www.faacanhelp.org

I found Jesus because of divorce. Wouldn't you rather find Him while married?

After salvation in the Lord, I connected the dots between the incest and romantic obsessions. The eating disorder calmed down, and all three ailments found their healing refuge and protection in the Lord. I re-emerged with a new Christian heart for my past marriage. Years after the divorce, I asked my children's father for a second chance. But my reconciliation attempts were rejected. I was "too Christian" for him now, which some might take as a compliment. But perhaps there were other reasons; maybe it was a lack of trust or hurt from the old wounds, and he was just trying to spare my feelings by being kind. Also, once you harm someone, it's very hard to reverse damage already done – why so many remarriages to the same person fail.

In response to this rejection, I began the selfish quest to find the right Christian man who would offer me marital redemption and evidence that divorce had been the right decision. I would find a believer and be equally yoked this time. Instead of dates, I had serial fiances, each feeling like a betrayal of the original marriage and only the last one leading to the altar a month after my father died in some weird grief response to avoid that pain. I found remarriage to be a sense of adultery so profound that I sought annulment five months into it, checking the unsound mind box on the court form. Only after I left did I discover for the first time a Scripture considering remarriage adultery. I had the conviction from my experience before I even read the Scripture.

> *"For example, a man who divorces his wife and marries someone else commits adultery. And anyone who marries a woman divorced from her husband commits adultery."*
> ~ **(Luke 16:18)**

I was stunned that my emotional experience of betrayal with remarriage preceded awareness of this Scripture, as if validation of a conviction I didn't even know I had. I wouldn't have believed it had I not felt the conviction so strongly *before even knowing of the Scripture* that I was cheating on the original marriage, but it was undeniable. Before I remarried, I even had a foreshadowing nightmare where we were in our own home, my original spouse and I. The new groom shows up at the door as an intruder. I don't let him in, saying, "You can't come in here. We're having a counseling session." In the dream, I closed the door. In real life, I let the man walk right in.

Would I have divorced had I known remarriage would be a closed door?

I also find it worth noting that I remarried someone in rapid response to my father's death. Likewise, it had been in reaction to my father's disowning me that I divorced. These coinciding junctures indicated that more was behind the behavior than I realized. Father issues drove my relationship issues. It meant my marital issues were not about my spouse, so neither were my divorce issues. My Heavenly Father showed me the Truth.

I finally got right with my original heart for the marriage before God again, though the spouse was no longer at the altar. Even reconciliation wasn't about remarrying, just like the divorce wasn't about him, either. Reconciliation was completely getting right with myself, my heart for the marriage, and right before God. Remaining unmarried has since been the holy and redeeming solution.

There was much more work ahead in the arena of regret. When I entered a new career in supervised visitation for non-custodial parents, I really learned how badly partners can treat each other. Not only was my childhood situation mild in comparison to those I encountered, but I found out that some couples who experienced adultery actually stayed married. I had left my marriage on the premise that I was *going to* commit adultery, not realizing I already had. All I know is, in the final analysis, I had given up too soon and divorced without legitimate reasons.

To make peace with this growing regret required serious consultation with the Lord. While I felt restored to wholeness, there was work to be done to help make things right for those affected. The regrets had to be turned into lessons for others as part of my reconciliation. Since my children went through our divorce, I didn't want them to become numb to its impact like I did. It was the denial of my own pain that made me insensitive to theirs before the divorce. I hope this book helps them, and you, avoid the same mistakes.

Divorce is not a "how-to-do-it-well" experience. Divorce is a bomb in the heart that goes off and leaves emotional wreckage for family members to pick up the pieces for the rest of their lives. Do the survivors heal and reassemble? Of course. But there are wounds that are untreatable without spiritual help, and only leave scars if they do close up. But so many people live with open wounds from divorce and go on to create further carnage in the marital world.

Despite my best efforts, I ended up repeating the divorce pattern from my parents and grandparents. In my marriage, I was missing a deeper experience of God and the necessary emotional sacrifice needed for my family.

Don't let this be the case for you.

So, my mission is to take this pain and turn it into something useful, maybe help prevent these bombs from going off in other families. As an unmarried woman, can my experience save others from divorcing? Would there be a way for me to write my way into the spaces of the lives of families and actually make room for them to work it out rather than duke it out? Could I minister to others in the same way I wished I'd been ministered to at the time, knowing what I know now? And best of all, I wondered if this wisdom could help steer my children clear of future potholes. Could I help them with my own failings?

My regret is real, but not because I didn't grieve properly, or because I couldn't "move on" or find the "right guy." No, it's because I walked away from the man God gave me – a mistake I wouldn't wish on anyone. I believe regret has a purpose when turned into lessons for others to learn from. This is how the Lord has used my remorse – to help keep others on their right path by sharing my experience of the impact of divorce on children.

Our daughters are now grown up, and I wonder what goes on in the hearts of children of divorce as they forge their adult relationships. None of mine are married yet. No referee is out there to pinpoint the moment the legacy of divorce would begin to call the shots, with or without their knowledge, in everything from how they handle conflict to how they communicate honestly. I can confidently say that our children are doing well today, but not because of the divorce or the job we did in co-parenting; rather, in spite of the divorce, they have overcome, adapted, and learned to move on. It's only to their credit, not ours, just like it was with me and my parents.

Yes, they've become who they are as a result of their experiences, but that never legitimizes divorce trauma. On any given day, for healing purposes, they'll gladly tell you about its devastating impact on their young lives. It's important not to evaluate your "success" as a divorced parent by the appearance of success in your children's lives. The impact divorce creates over the long haul doesn't care about anyone's success. Divorce is trauma, even if there is such a thing as doing it well. How they handle it or how it turns out is not an indication of whether you made the right choice. Rather, it's evidence of God looking out for them in spite of parents who don't. Divorce is always traumatic, painful, and life-altering for children. When there is a weak case for it, there is the most hope of preventing it with proper intervention.

May wisdom from my remorse convince your heart to let God shape your family legacy into the one He wants for you.

Prayer

Lord, I pray to know what You want for my marriage.

Questions

1. What is your story leading up to wanting a divorce?
2. Can you trace a "Point of Return" where you first "went wrong" in your marriage?
3. Who do you turn to for advice, support, and guidance?
4. What would it take for you to change your mind about divorce?
5. Do you lean on God enough?

Antidote #1

Averting the Prevailing Sadness

"The Lord is close to the brokenhearted and rescues those whose spirits are crushed."

~ Psalm 34:18

Divorce is the kind of loss that never really ends; it just keeps on losing. Look at the faces of the two kids on the cover of this book: my brother Alan, just 11 years old, and me, the girl at age 10. This was the summer our mother won her California Supreme Court case against our father, three years after the divorce. Even now, at 59, one simple heartbeat brings back the sadness of our childhood. I can assume that facial expression and be right back there. We moved to San Francisco for a year to be near the courtroom antics, during which we sat for five weeks one summer for an oil portrait mother commissioned from Tijuana artist Juan Badía for $5,000.[4] When she won their case, I made her a card, which I found in her legal files after she died. In blue marker: "We won our case!" That was the age I first learned to fake celebrating while being so sad. Somehow, this painting says it all.

---

[4] Silent Auction of the oil portrait to the highest bidder. Email soulcustody.pamela@gmail.com

I knew they were fighting over money, not custody. Dad gave Mom sole custody to take a job 3,000 miles away. My job was to alternately believe both sides of the story. When I was with Mom, I hated Dad. When I was with Dad, I hated Mom. This is how I earned their love and favor. Unable to show my conflict outwardly, all I did was hate myself and want to die. If Ghirardelli Square wasn't in town with 25-pound chocolate bars, sadness would have drowned me in the pool of our home at Gramercy Towers across the street from Grace Cathedral, where I was baptized.

Frozen in time, the sadness on our faces are the early signs of active alcoholism for both of us, which ended in 1988 for me and 1999 for him. If studies could prove, not just suggest, that divorce trauma leads to changing brain chemistry from all the fear, sadness, and rage, parents might re-examine quests for personal freedom. Then there's the lifelong blame. Our sad portrait bothered my father his entire life. After my mother included a photo of it in the Christmas card one year, he pointed to it as proof of her "bad job of mothering" from his home across the country, where absence somehow immunized him from blame or credit in parenting.

I purposely waited until all three parents died before publishing this book to not add to their guilt. Do you want your own children to spend their lives protecting you from yours? Divorce is one way to alienate your children and turn them into caretakers.

I wish my own childhood sadness was enough to prevent my adult decision to divorce with three children. Only years later did I feel the true nature of the emotional impact of divorce, once I stopped acting out. I wish someone, anyone, had sat me down before filing and said, "Let me explain to you the lifelong sadness you are about to instill into the hearts of your children without their knowledge or consent."

The sadness descends upon everybody affected. My children's father lost his own mother to cancer at 7, and now he has to see his daughters lose full-time access to their mom right as one of them turns 7. We tell our children they aren't losing us in divorce; it isn't true. Under the best of circumstances in shared custody, everybody's time is halved from here on out. The family, as you once knew it, is gone forever.

This prevailing, profound sadness is beyond the conscious level, and it is behind the unshed tears of children saying they're "fine." I lived with this sadness growing up, thinking it was normal. It felt like a tidal wave that never receded. Giant waves recurred in childhood dreams, not just because we lived by the beach. The best way to describe the effect of such sadness is that it takes away the child's security in joy. Joy is no longer safe, seemingly never again. Their ultimate security – the parents' marriage – is dissolved, and the pieces are everywhere. There is no psychic container to "hold" the child's joy, no foundation for it to grow or deepen. As it spreads, a cloud settles in, and things just aren't the same anymore. For the child, it's never the same again, which is a way of saying their original true joy in life is gone forever, and they feel it will never return. I used to pour this all out in my diaries: *It never goes away, and comes back really strong when someone leaves. Will I ever be happy again? It feels like forever. I'd only be happy if they got back together. Then I wouldn't be sad anymore.*

How come my own experience with it the first time wasn't enough to stop me from divorcing? I'm still baffled by this, 17 years later. I know this much, however: I was desensitized to the pain of my own childhood, which is what enabled me to be inconsiderate of my children's emotions. It didn't help that being on antidepressants and mood stabilizers had the side effect of less empathy from me overall.[5] I also felt immune from suggestions that spouses with bipolar disorder can be more prone to infidelity. Pride sounds like "That will never happen to me!" At

---

[5] Study by D.A. Harmer et al, Journal of Psychiatric Research, 2009.

the root of it all is childhood sadness, only to be compounded by a fresh round of trauma.

The first time I saw this prevailing sadness occur in my daughters was the night they left to stay in the new house he bought. We thought the novelty of staying in Papa's new house would be a good idea on her 7th birthday. But you can't really make a good thing out of a tragic occasion. Nor can you take a happy occasion and try to soften bad news with it. That night, I watched the spirit of two little girls go from 100 to 10 percent, unable to detect it in our baby. The birthday didn't prevent, avert or cover up the thick layer of sadness.

The divorce papers were in process. He bought a second house. But the divorce was not final yet. If I could have just seen that this sadness was not just an event, but an emerging way of life, I might have had the conviction I desire now: "This is the wrong thing to do." And there are these papers you can file in court to withdraw the divorce papers.[6] Never think divorce can't be reversed at any stage, except when the other spouse gives up on you and

---

[6] In California, for example, get divorce case dismissal forms at https://www.courts.ca.gov/forms.htm and search forms CIV 110 and 120.

remarries or dies. I mistakenly thought I was locked into a course of action.

It's baffling how smart you think you're being when you're making the biggest mistake of your life.

Visit a Divorce Support Group

One way to say "No, thank you" to divorce while there's still time is to ask to attend a divorce support group while you're still married. You can find them at churches, and some groups are for divorce prevention. Reading one divorce support group pamphlet might have been enough. These words alone may not have stopped me, but as I read them years afterward with full identification of their truth, they hit home:

"The pain and loss experienced during divorce can be characterized as a secret grief – a hidden grief that few people outside of the divorce experience understand. Divorce is unique because these feelings of loss and grief co-mingle with our most basic and profound human passions – love, hate, and jealousy. The diverse and intense feelings generated during this period include relief and utter devastation. Such emotions are often compounded by feelings of guilt, shame, abandonment, rejection, and failure. If not resolved, these dynamics may lead to a sense of personal inadequacy. Unresolved divorce issues can be practical, social, philosophical, and spiritual. People dealing with these issues often feel trapped, isolated, and alone."[7]

These are the same effects on children, to varying degrees. Chronically missing a parent – conversely, regularly missing your child – creates a despondency that sets in on a permanent basis, inherent in parental absence. It carves out a Grand Canyon in the soul. It digs a deep, dark hole in the soul that no one notices, not even the child, because they've fallen into it, and don't even know that's what happened.

Chronically missing a parent creates sadness, despondency, apathy, indifference, and loneliness in children. The slow build-up over time erodes their ability to identify and cope with these emotions. Not being able to identify the emotions creates a need for that space to be filled with something other than the very thing that is missing, in an effort to repress the horrifying inner reality, the black void that develops in their soul like a cancer.

It's very hard for a parent to see in advance that when with Mom, the child is always going to be missing Dad, and with Dad, the child is

---

[7] www.churchinitiative.org that created DivorceCare has a marital crisis intervention tool, "Choosing Wisely." I started offering it to married couples through Pathway Church in Redlands, CA, in 2025.

always going to be missing Mom. So you're creating a lifelong "can't have" situation that stirs up discontent, longing, and "grass is greener" mentalities. I had all of that growing up, and I was now passing it down.

Longing creates a preoccupation that undermines every task, from getting up in the morning to getting along with people, getting good grades, and doing good work. Longing makes you feel 10 percent off center, the grass always being greener elsewhere, and so it breeds discontent, jealousy, and fantasy that life would be better "when" and "if."

Dad left home when I was 7, and I was now imposing the same pattern on my 7-year-old daughter and her sisters by having her Dad leave home. Unconscious timing? Granted, he went across town, not the country, but *he still left home.* And now their father was in a separate home, too. They were angry at him for leaving the family home when I was the one who divorced him.

By divorcing as an adult, I recreated the same dynamic I had with my father – setting up a permanent distance and a lifelong longing for both me and all three daughters. They were a repeat of the dynamic of keeping father afar. At best, parents get 50/50 custody, which still reduces parenting presence to half-time.

Longing is a terrible emotion to inflict upon children. Our middle daughter, at age 7, would write to me at night in her diary from her father's house, telling me how much she missed me. One day, the diary entries just stopped, as if resignation had set in. They get so used to being without you that even if they have a need for you, they forget to express it. Because you were always there before, they didn't have to work so hard. But now they forget they need you, because you are no longer always there.

Growing up, I was obsessed with my father coming home or me going to live with them across the country. In my diary, I wrote a letter to them asking if I could come live with them, but I didn't send it or tell anyone. To me, it was the saddest moment of my childhood – this unsent letter, this deep longing subverted. As a result, the longing for "the unavailable man" formed, making me wonder if I recreated that longing again by divorcing, because there's no surer way of making your husband unavailable than to divorce him.

As a parent, your "off times" can get lost in work and the daily events that don't include our children's sphere, so we wonder why we lose touch with our children. The same chronic sadness from missing our children builds in us and causes us to reach for unhealthy things to fill the void. How tricky it is to maintain our connection with them, because the shallow words we grasp for don't really reach our children in their own state of bewilderment. We wonder why everything feels so surfaced because we can't get beneath it with any kind of meaningful consistency with the constant interruptions of divorced life. It's come and go and off and on.

You can't imagine yet how it feels to chronically miss your children on a regular basis, the unbearable pain of missing them day to day. *You will not be with them day in and day out.* This is hard to grasp when they've been in your sphere from the beginning. There are times you can feel like a visitor, a babysitter, or a family outcast — especially when your former partner builds a new family without you. You never again have the consistent day-to-day interactions of their childhoods. It is intermittent parenting for the rest of your life. Grandparenting won't be any different. Adult children are still forced to divide their time between two homes. Up front, you lose half your time with grandchildren you don't even have yet.

Proceeding with divorce, headed toward Club Thirty, your only salvation from feeling so alone is to become closer to the Lord. Because in other partners, you won't be able to find what only God can give. To long for the Lord is where longing belongs.

As the Psalmist says in Psalm 42: 2, 'I thirst for God, the living God. When can I go and stand before Him?'

I see now how the Lord could have filled that father vacancy in me and also helped me before I vacated the father of my children from the family home. I long for the Lord today, as He satisfies the longings of my soul that I once imagined someone else was supposed to provide. I was looking to the partner to provide what only God could, placing expectations on my spouse above and beyond the ability, necessity, and purpose of the marriage.

Marriage is to *serve God*, but I didn't look at it that way. My mindset was about what the marriage wasn't doing for me, rather than what I could do for the marriage and family. The marriage was forcing me to look at issues I didn't want to face. This inherent selfishness is no basis for growth, maturity, and holy matrimony. Straying was evidence my priorities were off. So I wish I'd waited it out, gotten out of those emotional affairs, and faced my own issues without ruining my marriage and family.

If God is missing in your case, the time to turn to the Lord is now, before you divorce, not after, when suffering from the effects of divorce leaves you in emotional rubble begging for God's mercy. Let God save you from becoming a member of Club Thirty. Don't break the heart of the family. Club Thirty members risk picking up the pieces of wreckage for the rest of their lives.

Staying for the Children is Wisdom

Judith Wallerstein, in her 25-year study of the lifelong impact of divorce on children, came to the conclusion that an unhappy marriage is better for children than a divorced one. Now deceased, she told *Newsday* in 1994: "What in many instances may be the best thing for the parents may by no means be the best thing for the children. It is a real moral problem. If parents could swallow their misery, they should stay together with their kids."

I only read her book *The Unexpected Legacy of Divorce* once I divorced, when it had no chance of preventing it for me. Mine wasn't even an unhappy marriage; I wanted to escape my own issues. I had convinced myself that what was good for the mother, would be good for the children. It didn't occur to me that I could be delusional about what was good for me. How about what's bad for the father would be bad for the children? That's the trouble with divorce: In a weak case, selfishness is at the root of it, and the person who wants out is only thinking of one person, not the family.

To think of the family first, you have to consider what marriage means to the children. Their married parents create a security blanket for them. Wrapped up in our own viewpoints, instead, we fail to see what our children gain from our being together, and therefore, we fail to see what divorce *takes* from them. And we certainly don't see the bond of our marriage from their perspective. We're too busy looking at the other person's flaws to notice the flaws in our thinking. *Children's entire worlds* depend on the two parents they've been used to since birth. That's why many will feel their lives are over at parental divorce. For them, their world falls apart.

Years before the divorce, our oldest child, then 7, asked: "Will you and Daddy ever get divorced?" With all my heart, I answered, "No!" I meant it. I felt it. How did I know it would turn out to be a broken promise? How betrayed she must have felt later. Why did I not feel any betrayal against my own previously loyal heart? This is the erosion of emotional affairs; they are a threat to the marriage. Now, more than ever, I wish I'd prayed on my knees and asked God to reveal His heart for my marriage.

What made my daughter wonder about divorce is another good question. If I had inquired what made her wonder that, I could have been given clues about her perspective of Mommy and Daddy. Whenever your children say something about your marriage, it's a sign that they see something long before you do as a couple. Young children, especially those around the age of four, known as the first adolescence, are extremely perceptive and honest. Later, this daughter would say, "I knew it was over 18 months before when you moved into separate bedrooms." Even I didn't know at the time, but she could see it coming. And she couldn't stop it, either. She recalls the time he searched for other houses on the computer while she closed the study door and barricaded it with stuffed animals to prevent him from leaving.

This daughter is 27 now and a clinical therapist. She went into therapy at age 10 during the divorce, and now she works with children and teens who've suffered trauma. I often wonder what occupation she would have felt free to pursue if it weren't for the influence of divorce. These are things we'll never get to know about our children's lives because divorce impacts everything from that one moment forward.

The time to think of putting the kids first is before divorce. Ever notice the first thing on some parents' minds once they're divorced? "Let's put the kids first." This sad irony occurs too late. Club Thirty parents wish they had put the kids first. If we put them first, we wouldn't have gotten divorced in the first place. We must put the children's happiness before our own, or we end up in Club Thirty. It's difficult to be a happy parent when you see your children so unhappy.

Before You Would Tell the Children…

"Those who control their tongue will have a long life; opening your mouth can ruin everything."
                                            ~ **(Proverbs 13:3)**

It's one thing to ask your spouse for a divorce, and quite another to inform your children of the decision. I didn't think long and hard enough before announcing it to them. I wished I'd never said a thing to them about it and worked out the urge to divorce in privacy. Because once we told them, it really felt set in stone. Now, I had to carry it through. It is so painful to tell children about divorce that most parents don't. My Dad was just gone one day, not a word.

From what I read online, 75 percent of parents talk to their children about their divorce for less than 10 minutes.[8] This is outrageous. Imagine your boss not telling you that your company is being sold. And that's not even family; it's business.

---

[8] Find more figures at momlovesbest.com, where Beth McCallum compiled 25 Children of Divorce Statistics & Facts, Feb. 18, 2025.

After much rehearsal in counseling, we told the three girls we were getting divorced. *It's the speech I regret most in my life.* After we told them, I'll never forget our daughters, ages 7 and 10, looking up at me in tears over their baby sister, only a year old at the time: "But Mommy, she will never get to see you both together!"

Why didn't I listen to that as the one main reason to stay? I still hadn't filed for divorce yet when she said this. But now it felt official because we let them know. The damage began in that conversation with the children. Their pleading expressions begged for there to be another way. My cold heart was impenetrable behind the fortress of what I was trying to hide from my own past and present. I should have sat down and really pondered what it meant that for her entire childhood, she would never know her parents as a unit in the same home. The other two wouldn't get that for the rest of their childhoods. It wasn't too late for us when she shared this observation. Only pride prevented a decision reversal. Why did I let my own issues get in the way of what was best for my family?

Back then, it was about being locked into a course of action no matter what the cost. I remember feeling decided and driven, as though nothing would deter me. Yet, all these years later, I heard her plea for the first time in a completely different way. Turns out my own children offered the best divorce advice of all: *Don't do it!* Why didn't I listen to them?

It was too late three years after the divorce, when that same baby, who then turned 4, had an inconsolable meltdown: "I want two parents in one house!" It was so loud that I wrote it down, followed by: "When I was a baby, you were in one house, and now!" Her sisters had been right.

It's easy to chalk off babies as not knowing what's going on, but they absorb and assimilate all the emotions of everyone else. And if you think she wouldn't be affected by the joy reduction, you're not understanding how babies react to people in their environment. This kind of wreckage leaves a broken, wounded, hungry space in children's hearts at all non-verbal levels.

To help with damage control, we held a family meeting:

> "You know Mommy and Daddy are not going to be married anymore. We are sad about that, and we know you are, too. We are living here together for now. Before that would ever change, we want you to know, first and foremost, that you will not be losing either of us. We are both here for you, always, as your parents. We have a strong parenting bond with each other that could never be broken. None of these adult changes in our relationship are your fault, or your

responsibility. We are taking care of ourselves, and we are here to take care of you no matter what happens. We can love you through all the worries and concerns you might have and hope you can continue to bring your feelings to us. We want to help you. Changes like this are difficult. We are still a family with a Mommy and Daddy, three beautiful daughters, three cats, and a kitten. Now, is there anything you would like to ask or share about now?"

Yeah, like...Why?

I don't even remember how we answered "why" back then. All I know is, reading this 16 years later, it feels cold and heartless. At the time, it felt like I was being honest and loving. Do you really want to give a speech like this to your children that you'll regret later? If you really want to feel the impact of how sad it is, re-read the script aloud as if you're trying those words on for size, pretending your children are in front of you. It makes me cringe today. I hope it's a deterrent for you and not a warm-up.

Doesn't it feel like one big lie: We're breaking up, but "We are still a family?" No matter how you sugar-coat it, there's no way to make it sound right. That's because it's wrong. Divorce itself is wrong when you're a future member of Club Thirty and don't know it. How can it ever be the right thing to do in circumstances where it isn't warranted? If I divorced with such lightweight, nonsensical outward reasoning, my guess is there are many others whose real reasons are just as selfish and also deeply hidden. These are the people I'm trying to reach in time before they make the wrong move. These are the people who still have time to reconfigure their view of marriage and keep their families together. I lacked the courage to face my past and present.

Before we gave this speech informally to our children, we should have sought input from religious counseling, and made our appeal to God. At least one of us could have reached out, and I think it might have been enough, at least for the courage to face myself.

If I could go back and rewrite the speech, I would. This alternate script was therapeutic to write – what I wished I'd said instead to retract or counter the decision:

> "You know we have been having troubles, but Mommy and Daddy are going to work it out. We have decided to remain married because we know it's the right thing to do and the best thing for you. We have a strong parenting bond that could never be broken, and we are working on making our marriage bond stronger. It became weak due to a lack of

spiritual sustenance. As we bring more faith into our lives, we know God will protect our family and lead us forward as a unit to overcome any obstacles ahead of us. With God's help, we will get through our fears, doubts, and challenges that have to do with our own personal histories. We will not let our adult histories dictate your future security as children. We will not let our adult failures determine the outcome of our family life. We pledge to stay together even during times we aren't getting along, and to pray for forgiveness and courage and perseverance to keep doing the right things for your well-being and ours."

These are wishful words today. Read this script aloud now if you like, to compare. Which speech feels right? If I could erase that family meeting we had where we let them know we weren't going to be married anymore, I would. I didn't know that would be our second to last family meeting– the last one informing them of Papa's new home. Later, family meetings would always be without their father, and on his end, they wouldn't include me. There was always something missing, always something lacking, always something less secure about it all. The family meetings post-divorce felt vainly self-sufficient, Mom trying to get by on her own without Dad. It changed somewhat once I found

Jesus, but they were never raised religiously, so my understanding of God never could catch up with them after divorce. Had I stayed married, I think I would have had a greater chance of seeing how the love of Jesus could have worked through me to uplift and support the family unit. But I'll never know because that's not what happened in my case during the marriage.

How helpless they must have felt that they couldn't stop the divorce from happening. What if they thought we didn't love them enough to stay together? Who knows what really goes on in the minds of our little children – all three of them acutely aware of the iniquity of it all?

Don't do this to your children. Feel the guilt of just thinking of divorce, now, while you're still married. Let the guilt of thinking of doing it keep you from doing it. In this way, guilt can be the driving motivator to stay. Otherwise, your guilt becomes the price of admission to "Club Thirty." Once you enter those doors, the guilt is on a different level and serves no purpose except to warn others of the dangers ahead. Remorse over the children can stay with divorce petitioners for a lifetime, and it can alienate the children whenever it comes up in conversation. It's no fun for children to see their parents feeling guilty and remorseful over anything.

I could have decided divorce was something I didn't want to put my children through. I wish I'd turned to anyone and said, "I can't do this to my children." But now, it's your chance to do better. This book is here to help save your marriage. One marriage saved is the goal of this book, and a track record of those helped will be kept if you email soulcustody.pamela@gmail.com to share your success story.

Prayer

Lord, fill my heart with Your presence. I only long for You.

Questions

1. Am I in a hurry to divorce? If so, why?
2. Have I considered the emotional impact of divorce on our children?
3. Divorce isn't an event; it's a process and a long-lasting trauma. Am I prepared to consciously choose this route?
4. Look closely at any doubts I have about divorce. They may have hidden lessons for me.
5. Think about what our children have said or asked about our marriage. Sometimes, God speaks through our children. Am I really listening?

Antidote #2
Restoring God's Covenant in Marriage

"But God made them male and female from the beginning of creation. This explains why a man leaves his father and mother and is joined to his wife, and the two are united into one. Since they are no longer two but one, let no one split apart what God has joined together."

~ Mark 10:6-9

As the Reverend Tom quoted this above Scripture for us on our wedding day, he tied our forearms together with a large knot of red fabric. *It didn't occur to me at the time to include myself in the "let no one" category; I'm thinking don't let anyone outside the marriage ruin the marriage.* To know what you're breaking up, first, you have to understand what you formed. And on August 19, 1992, at the Easy Does It Ranch in Philipsburg, Montana, God created one of the four happiest days of my life, shared with the births of those three daughters foreshadowed by baby's breath adorning the covered wagon prop.

If divorce was as easy as untying a knot, it wouldn't be so painful. After you have been made one flesh in the eyes of God, you don't just part ways. Instead of tearing a piece of paper, like the marriage license, it's tearing flesh. Unbeknownst to me, marriage made us "one flesh."

This is why *asunder* is a word worth noting, as in how it's used in this same Scripture in the

King James Bible: *What therefore God hath joined together, let not man put asunder.* If something tears or is torn asunder, it is *violently separated into two or more pieces.* Because I didn't understand "the one," I didn't understand how incredibly painful it is to be *torn asunder* from the one. Because I didn't experience "the one," I felt like we were two people together who could go their separate ways. And just because I didn't believe in the one flesh concept back then doesn't mean it wasn't true in conceptual reality. In fact, it was divorcing that revealed the true nature of the one flesh, when torn apart, by how it felt. You feel gutted, exposed, and vulnerable. Divorce is a soul shredder.

What you first think is a paper cut is torn flesh, after all, leaving carnage. This is not just for the couple but also for the children who witness it. Because the children formed from this union, they are also torn asunder. They go through things we can't even begin to imagine. I still don't know all the ways it affected them, and I'm not sure they do, either, to this day. It's especially elusive on the baby, now grown, who only had both parents together during her first year.

I didn't realize until far too late the serious nature of my wedding vows. Had I even once considered what my marriage represented to God under whom the contract was first made, I would have had a better chance. Marriage as a covenant between a man and woman honors God. It's a symbol of God's love for the church. He loves the church as a husband loves his wife. As a couple, they glorify God by showing what it means to love and serve others. Marriage reflects the unity and oneness of God, and this is what the children see.

We made a vow before God that we would stay married. It never once occurred to me in divorce mode that I was dishonoring the God contract. I thought I was doing God's will to leave. In my state of sin, I was unaware of even the need for a Biblical understanding of marriage. I didn't know how my infidelity was coloring my perception of my spouse and cutting me off from the experience of knowing God in the marriage.

Review your wedding vows. Revisit the history and heritage of your relationship. The time to reminisce on what first brought you together is *before divorcing.* Only long after salvation in Christ did I understand why, on my wedding day, I felt heaven on earth all day long, as if God Himself witnessed it. Most vivid in my mind is the baby's breath on a flower-covered wagon at the altar, predicting our three little girls. I thought about the history we had built from the day we met, how we wrote our own vows, and how a friend mowed our bridal path in the field. I remembered the matron of honor's toast at the table: "There will be no divorce," she said on video, raising her glass. Later, she and I both joined the two-thirds of women who petition for divorce.

Forbes Advisor reported a 2022 study showing that 72% of couples said they didn't fully understand the commitment involved in marriage before they tied the knot. One-third of couples believe they should have made more of an effort to prevent divorce. These are the ones who end up in Club Thirty.

I fully believe God would have healed our marriage had we turned to Him. But spiritual blindness kept us from seeing that. It reminds me of a verse from Matthew 13:15: *"For the hearts of these people are hardened, and their ears cannot hear, and they have closed their eyes – so their eyes cannot see, and their ears cannot hear, and their hearts cannot understand, and they cannot turn to me and let me heal them."*

This blindness, in part, was due to a lack of a religious foundation in our marriage; and I think that might have helped. We spent lots of money in premarital counseling talking about communication and boundaries, but we didn't even go for free pastoral counseling. I don't remember having one conversation about God, our faith in Him, His will for our marriage, the contract we made, the vows we said, let alone the one flesh concept. Our premarital counseling wasn't through church, so we didn't touch on God's role. I never sought God's opinion on my leaving the marriage. In my own counseling, I talked only about God's will being that I leave the marriage. Once I decided I wanted out, nothing that contradicted my mission even entered my mind, nor did I seek to be challenged. I don't recall anyone ever questioning my decisions, though my therapist strongly advised not divorcing while pregnant.

I looked for successful divorce role models and learned divorce is strangely contagious. I was inspired and encouraged by my best friend's divorce. I borrowed her copy of the book *The Good Divorce*. That title is like saying there is such a thing as a good death. I collected books on how to do it well. I'm here now to challenge your decision before you end your marriage, like I wish someone had done for me.

The book I wished I'd read instead is by the late Timothy Keller: *The Meaning of Marriage: Facing the Complexities of Commitment with the Wisdom of God*. Here are three gems from it: 1. We are to live for the other, 2. We can't look to our spouse for what only God can do, and 3. Wedding vows are not a declaration of present love, but a mutually binding promise of future love. Write these three tenets down; they might just save you from filing for divorce.

Doubts Can Strengthen Faith

"Each time he said, "My grace is all you need. My power works best in weakness." So now I am glad to boast about my weaknesses, so that the power of Christ can work through me."
~ (**2 Corinthians 12:9**)

At the time, I didn't see it, but the trial period at that critical 13-year point was a call to a stronger marriage, not evidence of a broken one. The real breaking point of our marriage was when we got divorced, not before. The growing infidelity and adultery in the heart weren't signs of a broken marriage; they *were* the flaws (the broken parts). And the issues driving them in me were the deeper root of the problem on my end as the petitioner.

When people about to divorce say, "Our marriage ended years ago," they have no clear understanding of what's to come when it actually does end. Not an active, believing Christian at the time before divorce, I was not on guard to protect my marriage. I didn't understand how marriages come under spiritual attack by the enemy.

The fragility of marriage itself is not a sign of weakness; it's a sign that God is present in all His glory. The stronger the attacks on the marriage, the more evidence the enemy opposes the strength of the union in God. It's an invitation to go deeper, not run for the hills. So consider your trials evidence that you've got a really good thing going in the eyes of God, and all you need is God's grace to endure.

I wished I'd asked for grace, for myself, for my husband, for the children, for the marriage, and for the family. Ask for grace! Ask for it now. Let there be plenty of room for the Grace of God to permeate the home life from top to bottom.

Grace returns when someone repents. What does it mean to repent?

Jesus spoke of repentance in Matthew 3:2: *"Repent of your sins and turn to God, for the Kingdom of Heaven is near."* Repentance isn't just a prayer; it's a change of heart and direction. It didn't matter that I didn't know that divorce was wrong at the time I did it. I still had to get right with God, and salvation itself did not make regret go away. I had work to do. Repentance requires an admission of guilt for committing a wrong or for not doing the right thing, followed by a promise or resolve to not do it again, followed by an attempt to make restitution for the wrong, or, in some other way, reverse the harmful effects of the wrong where possible. Repentance involves reviewing one's actions, feeling contrition or regret for the wrongs, and then actions that demonstrate a change for the better. Contrition is a powerful word; it invites

Godly sorrow for our actions, true sorrow about them that changes us.

As 2 Corinthians 7:10 tells us, *"For the kind of sorrow God wants us to experience leads us away from sin and results in salvation. There's no regret for that kind of sorrow. But worldly sorrow, which lacks repentance, results in spiritual death."* We must move beyond surface-level regret. So don't stop at mere regret. Touch the Godly sorrow within for the ways you've departed from the marriage to this point, whatever they may be in your case, followed by thanksgiving. You haven't yet taken that disastrous step toward ending the union: filing for divorce.

Godly sorrow floods in when you even just get a glimpse of how your behavior in the marriage may be affecting your children. Could I do it all over again? I would grab God, extricate myself from those emotional affairs, and run to my husband and beg for forgiveness. Then I'd go hug my three children silently saying to myself, "I'm sorry I almost left your Daddy." All that time I spent preoccupied and distracted could have been attention paid to my spouse and children. But I lost even more time with them all when it resulted in divorce.

When I got divorced, I became a living example of this Godly sorrow Scripture. One of the most surprising things about divorce was the spiritual disillusionment that first comes with it. I didn't turn to God for help while married, but suddenly, I had no problem complaining to Him about the results of divorce. I didn't call on Him to stop me, but I was now calling on Him to stop the pain. My so-called freedom was a thinly veiled disguise. The grief flooded in:

Why would God give me this marriage, and then it would not work out?

Why didn't God stop me?

Why didn't God keep us together?

Why is God letting me go through divorce again?

My worst fears of repeating divorce had just been realized, and I was the one who set it in motion. At the time, I had no understanding of the nature and consequences of my sin – both the infidelity as well as the nature of divorce as being traumatically sinful "just because" I wanted out.

Even a full-on salvation by Jesus didn't wipe the inordinate guilt from my soul that divorce levied. Only writing this book is showing me the ultimate relief from it – a mission to save other marriages from the same mistake by sharing the lessons learned.

I found some relief from blaming God when I separated the effects of human sin from the nature of God. I still wish God had stopped me from divorcing, but I had no solid relationship to ask Him to stop me, at the time. I even blamed God for not making it clearer at the time that I needed Him – as if my conflict and turmoil weren't enough of a sign.

Loud and clear, I wish someone had told me: *"It's not God's will that you divorce."* Equally as bold, I needed to hear over and over: *"Don't expect your spouse to do for you what only God can do."*

I justified leaving the marriage as it was God's will. While concessions for divorce are made in the Bible, divorce isn't what God intends for couples. Divorcing in weak cases is unnecessary when you consider that Christ died for our sins. His finished work at the cross made it so that we could live free of sin and in His love. The answer is in the Grace of God, not divorce. I admire the many couples who take long and hard, honest looks at their marital troubles and end up staying married because of it.

Marriage forces suffering for healing purposes. We have to outgrow the pains that are already inside of us. There's suffering for healing purposes, and then there's optional suffering. To opt for optional trauma by divorcing when there is already so much that already comes our way unintentionally, internally, and accidentally in life, just seems unwise. Who would choose trauma? But, to be in control of events in my life that I wanted to deny, I created my own suffering and provided more for others at their expense. I didn't have to, when Jesus had already paid the price for my freedom from ruin. I just didn't know it in time.

None of this made sense to me overnight. I had to keep asking the questions. Why all this betrayal? I had to look further into my history for clues. What I came up with explained it enough. I also blamed God for taking my father from me. And I blamed *her,* the wicked stepmother...

August 13, 2024

Fifty years ago today, I can recall the wedding of my father and new stepmother as the start of a burning jealousy and betrayal that set the tone for the rest of my life. I was 8 years old. Jealousy started that summer day in 1974; envy better describes the evil nature of it. Jealously usually doesn't occur for children regarding the relationship between their *biological* parents, unless one parent commits incest and incites it. Otherwise, children love to see the love between their biological parents. No, this seething dynamic arises with step-parents. They are competition, interlopers, and most of all, "not my Mom or Dad." When couples violate the remarriage Scripture, it's most intense. We leave it up to the child to get used to it and ignore the reason they feel so wronged, which is often because it *is wrong* in many situations.

Fifty years later, I can still feel the unfairness of their union from the start. I see it now from the adult perspective: my parents were supposed to be married before I even arrived, and stay married. Children aren't supposed to be seeing weddings; they come along after them. She was "the other woman," particularly so in my case of incestuous emotional attachments to my father that were not my doing or my fault.

Years after my own divorce and when my youngest daughter turned 12, I set in motion the same betrayal for her when I remarried for five months. Hers was worse, though, because I had promised her just a few months before the wedding that it would be just mama-daughter time here on out at home, wanting to put her first, and other men nowhere. Six months later, I moved her into a strange man's home with me. At least my Dad didn't pull the "it's just you and me, kid" line and pull the rug out from under me. Five months into it, after an annulment, massive apologies, and a move back to the original home we had, my promise was back in gear, but the damage had been done at her tender age. Undoing the harm was the best I could do. It's better to back up and get on the right track again than to have too much pride to throw it in reverse and continue down the wrong path.

The tragic point I'm trying to make here is, once again, I was inconsiderate of how my behavior would affect other people before making sweeping decisions that include them. It's not that I was purposely choosing to be mean. A selfish heart just doesn't think of others. The tragedy is in not thinking of these things first. So, I'll ask you: Do you want to open up future avenues of jealousy and betrayal for your children? Because the insecurity that divorced life brings can seriously undermine daily family life. And these emotions can set in motion behaviors in your children that you wouldn't think would occur. As in my case, I didn't think I'd have such a lifelong layer of betrayal impacting my life from that 1974 wedding day forward.

I look back now for the integrity I wished I'd had. Since I felt this way at age 8, had I known it was a set up for me to be a betrayer myself, I might have questioned myself back then like I do now. I would not have wanted to repeat the same dynamic on my own child. I would have made a conscious attempt not to repeat the same betrayal dynamic.

Payback occurs naturally for the cheater when the spouse that got left goes on to become happily remarried. But ask any parent who regrets divorce and they'll also tell you it feels like the other new person assumed the place that was once yours. Your children have a separate family life and you're not in it. And because divided time continues into the next generation, grown children are still forced to navigate two homes once they have their own. You're never grandparents in one home, after divorce.

And if you don't go on to form your own new family, you're like the lone parent all the children have to worry about, especially as you age. It's an unfair burden to put on them as a single parent. You're transferring your original wedding vow of caring for your former spouse in sickness and in health, to your children, making it their responsibility. Our American culture doesn't support being unmarried. But it supports rampant remarriage, with a 60 percent failure rate to go along with it.[9] Yet another example of the loss that keeps losing.

The overwhelming impact of divorce is too much to bear alone. In moments of pain and confusion, we often cry out, *"God, are you listening?"* At one point, the disciples asked

---

[9] Pew Research Center, 2014.

Jesus, *"Teach us to pray,"* and He replied to pray in this manner:

> *"Our Father in heaven, may your name be kept holy. May your Kingdom come soon. May your will be done on earth, as it is in heaven. Give us today the food we need, and forgive us our sins, as we have forgiven those who sin against us. And don't let us yield to temptation, but rescue us from the evil one."*
>
> **~ (Matthew 6:9-13)**

This prayer is simple yet deep. It takes a miracle to save a marriage, but only a prayer to change your heart to be ready to receive one.

You can pray this short prayer: *Lord, please reveal where I cast blame on You. Help me not use You to build my case for divorce.*

As David cried out in Psalm 139:23-24, *"Search me, O God, and know my heart; test me and know my anxious thoughts. Point out anything in me that offends you, and lead me along the path of everlasting life."*

This is us letting God into our vulnerability to fix our heartache. It's not just about asking God to change our circumstances, but to change us, to reveal the ways we might be resisting His will or holding onto anger and bitterness. In asking for healing, we must first open ourselves to His refining work. We can let God save our marriage.

The Word on Marriage

Turns out I had the Bible in my home since my first wedding anniversary, but never availed myself of its power during the entire 16 years married. We never once opened the book together. How about you as a couple? Does parenting leave any room to sit down and read the Word together? It takes a few minutes. It's a vision I never experienced firsthand, but I had it right in my own home.

In early summer, I would start thinking about our wedding anniversary gifts, because we followed the annual gift-giving traditions. So, in year one, for "paper," my husband found me this giant antique Bible, which was bound in hard leather with clasps on it. He found it in Montana, where we were married. The Bible symbolized the potential of our marriage, but like I said, we didn't once ever crack it open in 16 years together. So, we never experienced the power of the Word in our marriage. In a fit of post-divorce disillusionment, I donated it to the Smiley Library in Redlands, which probably sold it in the book auction, which means someone has my Bible out there right now. *I'd like to buy it back from the one who has it. Original price: $119. I'll offer you $200 for it. I regret giving it away!*

Do you have a Bible on your shelf that you've never read? Find your Bible. Go get it right now, if you know where it is in the house. Open it to Mark 10:9. Those whom God has joined, let no one separate, *not even me.* This is how it speaks to me today. I forgot to include myself in the "others."

Spend time with Mark 10:9. Let it speak to you. Let it confuse any selfishness in your heart. Let it distract you from your personal agenda against your spouse or the marriage. It had the answers that I needed, because it had the power that I lacked. The verse contains the power to stay married.

If God Hates Divorce, Shouldn't I?

The Bible has some powerful and challenging words on the subject of divorce. One of the most gripping verses comes from Malachi 2:16: *"For I hate divorce, says the Lord, the God of Israel. To divorce your wife is to overwhelm her with cruelty, says the Lord of Heaven's Armies. So guard your heart; do not be unfaithful to your wife."* While meant to address unfair divorce practices among the people at the time, this Scripture caused me to want to find out how God views divorce. So, it was five years after the divorce, but I still wanted to make things right by retracing my steps. It was part of getting right with God. I discovered that God values marriage and wants couples to work toward healing, restoration, and reconciliation. I realized that what God hates is the pain and brokenness resulting from divorce, leaving families fragmented and vulnerable. To make sense of this Scripture, I didn't have to look further than my own life. *I hated my parents' divorce growing up. So why would I pass this hateful experience on to my children?*

All I have to do is think back to the terrible strain that overcame my family after my Dad left home. My mother was never the same. She worked twice as hard, drank twice as much, and pursued all kinds of unsavory characters. I followed in her footsteps in different ways, but used the template. They fought incessantly, for decades.

This is a memory of parental divorce from my diary as an adult in 1994:

> *"I'm hiding in the empty bathroom cupboard away from the kitchen where it's happening. It's black inside, self-contained like a cocoon. I try to shut out the noise – the only sound of my mother screaming on the telephone about money. The other side of it is silence to me. I hear her screeches and then the seagulls at the beach. I hate it when my mother screams, the vibrations severing my nerves like a knife. Inside the musty cupboard, I play with the half side of the toilet paper roll. My mother is nowhere but everywhere; her voice is the*

house. She has no idea where I am, listening as she competes with the seagulls for the empty space in my heart."

I have only one memory of my parents being together: a profound sense of parental security. I'm not sure how old I was, but one night, I crawled between my parents to sleep between them. In that ultimate sense of protection, I felt a security I was never going to match until I found the Lord. It turned out to be just one moment of my childhood. I'll never know what I actually did miss by not having two parents stay together.

Long into my own marriage, I also abhorred divorce. I spent years undoing the impact of my parents' divorce so it wouldn't affect my marriage. *So, how could I suddenly lose the conviction that it was wrong? Where and when did I start believing that divorce was okay, let alone an option?* Based on my knowledge of Scripture now, unless you vigilantly guard your heart against the threats to marriage, it's far too easy to succumb to lies, especially without the benefit of a belief in God that wants your marriage intact. That's what the Bible says in Proverbs 4:23, *"Guard your heart above all else, for it determines the course of your life."*

I didn't experience the Lord then like I do know. And that's my only explanation as to why divorce became an option and then a mission. It just slowly crept into my consciousness as a valid action, and it went unchallenged all the way through to the final decree. I justified it with a lot of nonsense about me being a better mother apart. I rationalized that divorce would be okay because we would be nice to each other and still take really good care of the kids together, separately. I had no idea about the true consequences.

Philippians 4:11-13 says, *"Not that I was ever in need, for I have learned how to be content with whatever I have. I know how to live on almost nothing or with everything. I have learned the secret of living in every situation, whether it is with a full stomach or empty, with plenty or little. For I can do everything through Christ, who gives me strength."*

The point of this Scripture applied to marriage is to weather both phases of contentment and discontent, so don't let your troubles shoot you out the door. It reminds us that contentment isn't just about having things go smoothly; it's about being at peace no matter the circumstances. Christ can care for it all, enabling you to stay and take care of your family. In my case, divorce was an emotional response driven by unresolved issues making the decision for me.

The barometer for whether you have a weak case for divorce is something that our society should measure before people file for divorce. It's too easy to get a divorce in the United States, for one. And like buying a gun, there should be a waiting period, only much longer than, for example, the 10-day gun law in California. If someone wants to file for divorce in California, it should be a six-month waiting period before they can, with required marital counseling of at least five sessions.[10] It should be much harder to get a divorce, as contrary as that sounds to our pursuit of happiness. Getting divorced when there is cooperation in California is as easy as getting married. Divorce can take six months to plan and finalize, and even weddings take longer than that to plan and execute.

I didn't have Jesus in my life then, but I do now. And I wonder how it would have been if I had come to Christ while still married. If you haven't either, would you like to? I'll offer you a simple prayer you can say.

---

[10] www.beforeyoudivorce.org, "Choosing Wisely," a marriage crisis intervention tool in five sessions for use in church settings. Videos and workbook intended for a facilitator to work with one couple.

Seek Him First

"They replied, 'Believe in the Lord Jesus, and you will be saved – you and your household.'"
~ **(Acts 16:31)**

I wish I had turned to the Lord as a Counselor, sought Him first. Or even if I just got closer to Jesus, I'm sure I would have seen my marriage through a different lens. Obviously, I was blind and couldn't see what was at stake.

I've said these words to you now. If you haven't tried turning to the Lord, now's your chance. He works miracles in marriages.

Many friends tell me that divorcing was the way I discovered my need for God. But I would like to think one could discover the need for God while married – that it wouldn't take a divorce to demonstrate a need for God. How about a struggling marriage as a sign of the need for God? Besides, how about all the other Christians out there, married, who already turn to God and still consider divorcing? What about them? I see now I could have turned to God when I started doubting the relationship. Little did I know my doubts were caused by my own behavior.

I thought I had enough of a God relationship. I didn't even question my relationship with God. That's because it wasn't the kind of relationship then with God that I would have thought possible. I didn't experience the Lord then like I do now, so I think there are many other parents out there just like me.

Three years after the divorce, I found myself at a Christian retreat in awe of the married couples who practiced forgiveness over affairs and managed to stay married. Even when they had a Biblical reason to divorce, they chose to stay! I left my marriage just on the notion of wanting the affairs to materialize, and even when he forgave me for that, I couldn't back up. I had entered the marriage with the idea that it would be over if either of us cheated, so I had absolutely no grace, no forgiveness, no room for error.

What does Jesus have to do with it?

> *"This means that anyone who belongs to Christ has become a new person. The old is gone; a new life has begun! "*
>
> ~ **(2 Corinthians 5:17)**

Salvation in Jesus Christ occurred for me five years after the divorce. It was a binge eating disorder that led to me reaching for Jesus, but the addiction to food was a result of unresolved divorce pain, guilt, and grief. So empty from overeating, I felt devoid of God. To be free of the addiction, I turned to Him in the forelight on May 15, 2013 during a phone call with a Christian woman in my 12-step food fellowship who led me through prayer to accept Christ. Writing about it in *"The Resting Place, A Graveside Diary"* helped me heal the divorce pain. It opened up a world of experiencing the love of Jesus that I had somehow not let into my life before.

While salvation wiped clean the sins, it left grief work to be done. I had to forgive myself where I never had before, and I had to seek forgiveness from the children and their father for making the wrong decision because I saw now, for the first time through Christian eyes, that I had not acted in love, that it was not the right thing to do, and that I wanted to make restitution.

It was salvation in the Lord that caused the change in my heart toward my marriage. That's why if you're a self-defined Christian who also hasn't accepted Christ as your personal savior, you have a chance at this same heart-changing epic life decision – before you divorce.

Why did it take that long and all that to cause me to turn to the Lord? I wish someone had squared me off back then and said, "You need the Lord. Why don't we give Him a chance? I could lead you in a prayer right now if you'd like to give your life to Christ." This did happen, just five years after the divorce.

You can turn to Christ now. You can collect your array of emotions, conflicts, history, past abuses, addictions, sins, behavior, and thoughts and leave them all at the foot of the cross. If you can't think of any one thing to bring, just bring your selfish or broken heart if you feel you have one.

Let the pain of your current situation come forward now, as you're reading. Collect it all. It's there to bring you closer to the Lord. That's what the suffering is meant to do – help you find your relief in Him. It may be the pain in your marriage or your personal history affecting your marriage that is calling Christ to be your Savior.

Jesus died for all of it so that you may live free and trust His love to run your life. *He died for our sins so that you don't have to keep living in them or punishing yourself for wrongdoing.* Can you feel relief just reading this? Perhaps the strain you have felt in your marriage is just calling you to God, a closer relationship with Him. If you have not accepted Christ before in your life, I'd like to give you a moment to do this now. If you've already experienced salvation, please reaffirm your faith by reading the prayer, and take a moment instead to pray for all the other parents who need salvation in Christ and who are also reading this prayer aloud for the first time.

Salvation in the Lord goes a long way to helping a marriage. When God is at the heart of a spouse's experience, it's like you stop looking to the marriage to do what only God can do, and selflessness expands. I could have turned from my emotional affairs and turned to the Lord to stop the behavior.

Here are the simple words you can say aloud, with me as your witness:

"Dear God, I know I'm a sinner and have fallen short of Your glory. I repent of my sins and ask for Your forgiveness. I believe that Jesus Christ is Your Son, who died on the cross for my sins and rose again on the third day. I invite Jesus into my heart and life, and I accept Him as my Lord and Savior. Please cleanse me from all unrighteousness and fill me with Your Holy Spirit. Help me to live a life that honors You and follows Your teachings. Thank You for loving me and saving me from sin and its consequences. In Jesus's name, I pray. Amen."

If you just now invited Christ into your heart, you can mark the date right here in this book:_____. Congratulations! Tell your spouse and children, tell a trusted friend, go to church, find a Bible study, and let the Holy Spirit guide your steps now in this marriage journey. See if your spouse will get religious counseling with you; if not, you can go yourself. Many doors can open now, and they will. You've given yourself a new foundation. There is still work ahead, but now you have God's love in your own heart to help.

God's love brings patience, fortitude, forgiveness, unselfishness, grace, compassion, and empathy, a feeling of everyone being cared for, and he can heal what's hurting.

Yes, I wish someone had led me to Christ while I was still married. After the divorce, I turned to food instead of God, and turning to God to be set free of the food uprooted what drove that addiction — self-centeredness and selfishness — grounding me in His love.

God has transformed my selfishness into God-centeredness. I get to live in this grace today, both as restitution toward the family and for a life infinitely more rich and satisfying in Christ. I have the right mindset now! I just wish it didn't take me losing my marriage to discover this. I don't think God was late in my case; apparently, He knew I'd return back to this juncture, in search of other married parents before it's too late.

If your spouse is a non-believer or distanced from Christianity like mine did before we met, Scripture says to stay put if you are the believing spouse. You can pray for your spouse's salvation or their return to the Lord. You can ask if your spouse will pray with you regardless of his or her belief.

Now that we've laid a foundation for spirituality or established there has been a lack of one, let's move on to the honesty required to stay married. By letting God into your heart in a significant way, and creating a relationship with Jesus, you have the power of the presence of God on your side. It can help keep your family together.

Get Honest

Humiliating, maybe, but I could have revealed my diary's secrets in marriage counseling. I hadn't done any physical harm yet; they were all at the thought level, and could have been aired in honesty, maybe even making room for discussion about the issues or putting an end to the obsessions before I physically acted out on them.

There were other junctures where my honesty was called for, and I remained silent until now. I could have un-done a contract I made as a 15-year-old with my first boyfriend. From a Christian standpoint now, I didn't realize how damaging it was to any future marriage. *Lord, take this verbal contract and shred it!* Here's what happened:

When I was 15, I decided to have sex for the first time with my first boyfriend. Only in hindsight do I wish I'd waited. I believe now that having sex too early and outside of marriage weakens the future marriage commitment. In my case, I made a verbal contract with that first boyfriend. We decided that if we were married to other people in the future, we could get together and it wouldn't be adultery because we decided to do it even before we were married. This transcendent view of "it doesn't count" was more serious than I thought. He was one of the three obsessions that ruined my marriage. How undermining this innocent pact turned out to be.

In premarital counseling, I could have brought this up as something to work out before I got married. I could have broken the age 15 contract with the other man. I also had chances to deal with it while married and before divorce. With a dose of honesty in marital counseling, I could have put an end to the pact, an end to the three emotional affairs, saved my soul, saved my marriage, and, most importantly, spared the little children from divorce.

We had two chances at pastoral counseling for marriage, before getting married and again when we started to have trouble as a married couple. Some churches offer year-long premarital counseling programs. Because I was on such a fast track to divorce to be "as quick and painless as possible," I carved out my own marital death sentence on sheer speed.

With Jesus in my heart, I had a love for the marriage and the man that only Jesus could ignite. It had been missing. And while it amplified my love for all people, it showed me just how beloved a spouse he was. It was just too late.

Prayer

Lord, thank You for my salvation and for the reinforcing strength, guidance, and power You've given me, my spouse, and my children at this vulnerable time. I trust the Holy Spirit is at work in our marriage and family. Amen.

Questions

1. Is there anything I'm looking for my spouse to provide that only God can provide?
2. Is there anything I need to admit to my spouse?
3. Do I have any prior commitments or contracts made verbally or otherwise with any other person other than my spouse?
4. Has my counseling included religious discussion on the meaning and commitment of marriage?
5. Have I prayed with my spouse about our marriage?

Antidote #3
Overcome Anxiety Through Prayer and Faith

"Don't worry about anything; instead, pray about everything. Tell God what you need, and thank Him for all he has done. Then you will experience God's peace, which exceeds anything we can understand. His peace will guard your hearts and minds as you live in Christ Jesus."
~ Philippians 4:6-7

Jesus can take the edge off your marital anxiety. If you think your current family strain is bad, you're just not aware of how much worse it could be once divorced.

It's hard for any parent to imagine the shock waves of anxiety that divorce sends through the bodies of small children. Chronic, debilitating, and far-reaching, it becomes part of their growing up. Anxiety sits like a puzzle piece on top of the sadness and serves as a way to prevent being overcome by the loss. Ironic as it sounds, anxiety protects the sadness and provides a sense of being in control of the never-ending feelings of not being in control or feeling that anyone else is in control. As overwhelming as divorce is for adults, children don't have the facts or information their parents have, adding to the confusion factor for children, which doubles when parents' stories differ. Anxious parents are also less able to help anxious children.

A lot of anxiety comes from discussing marital issues when children are in earshot. In the wake of its destruction, divorce seems to break down even the healthiest of boundaries against divulging too much information and saying things that don't need to be said. Confusion provides the most anxiety, as there are things adults don't say about their troubles, leading children to come to conclusions they are at fault for all kinds of unrelated reasons.

For children, their anxiety changes with their growing years. So, the divorce is at one age, but they experience the divorce dynamic and resulting impacts at all the ages into adulthood. I know this because I heard my three children ask the divorce questions in different ways over and over as they matured throughout their childhood, still trying to process the trauma. They'll likely keep asking at different stages in life – when their own marriages or parenthood come along. I'm wondering why my education in early childhood studies three years before the divorce did nothing to alert me to the enormous impact that divorce would have at every age. At every age and stage, children have to re-process and retell the story of divorce, carrying it around like a heavy backpack they have to unload each time a new person in their sphere asks about their parents or childhood.

My 1-year-old's impact didn't show until age 4 in that meltdown I told you about earlier: "I want Mommy and Daddy in one house like when I was a baby!" Infants are like little sponges. Toddlers feel anxiety over their basic needs being met, new custody or visitation schedules, where they're going to live, and even food they're going to eat. Fears arise of losing parental love, and where they'll sleep. As they age, add anxiety around money, food, and losing both parents. Into the pre-teen years, add feelings of disloyalty between parents and fears of being replaced by new partners. Into their teen years, they feel embarrassment about their family situation and can fear for their own future relationships ending in divorce. Young adults face anxiety about having to care for their single parents; they might rush into or avoid marriage, and they face financial and commitment anxiety.

Here's the biggest shocker from a study called The Longevity Project. *Children of divorce have a shorter life span of about 5 years compared to intact families.*[11] How horrifying. I didn't take the time to learn how they measured that, but I just wish someone had *told* me that. If

---

[11] The Longevity Project, Howard Friedman, Ph.D, and Leslie R. Martin, Ph.D, 2012.

that one statistic alone doesn't stop you, only a miracle can.

The Pinball Machine

Imagine this: Once divorced, your children move between you as parents like they're in a pinball machine. Instead of all coming to you from one direction, toward you both, their communications and life motions are now back and forth between you two. Sketch the directional lines on a piece of paper with the child as the starting point, and it looks stunted, frenetic, and confused, rather than forward and back to themselves and forward again. It could even short-circuit their emotional well-being. I think there should be more research into how this back-and-forth relationship with both parents affects a child's brain development.

If you're having a hard time picturing this, let me describe it another way, but from your perspective. They're always leaving you and coming to you again, going away and coming back. But you never find out the other half of the story. They could be coming to you both for the full story, and going out to lead their lives, but they're back and forth between houses trying to make both homes add up to their one life.

It's important to grasp this dynamic, so let me describe it a third way, this time from their perspective, and maybe yours too, if you recall from childhood divorce. I had to go back and forth between my parents, instead of once to both parents, trying to get my parenting. It became up to me instead of being led by them. Sure, they decided the custody and visitation schedule, or at least the courts did. But it suddenly became a job and a chore to make sure I was on the same page, deal with their incongruencies and opposites, ferret out who was telling the truth, and interpret different sets of parenting advice on the same topic. Now, I had potluck parenting instead of a main course. It left me overwhelmed, empty, and hungry.

The fourth scenario and the end result is that divorce can be so dysfunctional that children give up on getting their needs met by parents. They parent themselves and start to parent the siblings, as mentioned earlier. The pinball machine misfires, and the game shuts down. They don't go to either parent. The ball becomes still, rolls to the bottom, and stops. Another need for parenting arises, and they shoot off into the gameboard again, bouncing back and forth until their answer is achieved, but forever feeling they're playing this divorce game that never ends. And when they have children, they know they'll have to continue the back and forth between parents, with their own children along for the ride this time.

There's the trapping of "a loyalty bind." This is a trap children get into between their parents where they have formed an alliance with one or the other parent, usually at the parent's invitation and cultivation, for one and against the other. It also occurs in remarriages, with the loyalty between mom and the new step-mom or dad and the new step-dad.

Whereas the courts recognize that children are allowed to align with both parents, children become stuck feeling permitted alliance with only one, and parents push their agendas. It's complicated, unfair, and imbalanced, and my own experience growing up, taught me early in life to hide my feelings of love and also lie about them and deny them.

The reverberation of divorce is a sort of syndrome I've named Post Divorce Destruction Disorder, a layman's variation of the official post-traumatic stress disorder. Breaks of all kinds are set into motion – quitting jobs, moving homes, failed second marriages, relationship breakups, addictions, becoming ill, dangerous lifestyle risks physically and financially, social isolation, academic failures, fill in the blank. It's not just a divorce; it's the repetitive syndrome of breaks, from God, from oneself, from family members, from former friends, and what we least expect, breaking off from our children in ways we can't imagine. I made up the term for my first book, defining it in parents as "rapid weight loss in the initial radioactive phase of divorcing, perhaps coinciding with a rebound relationship, and leads to weight gain due to fierce attempts to bury grief and anger, while at the same time warding off the opposite sex in case that doesn't work out either."

The divorce version of PTSD brings about unexpected addictions and other self-destructive or uncharacteristic behaviors that could surprise even the most upstanding of mothers, as I felt myself to be. For example, breast augmentation was totally out of character for me, but I did it in a PDDD episode, right in the middle of the 2008 recession. Aside from the obvious financial stupidity, the reason that this "enhancement" is really destruction in disguise is that implants make it harder to detect breast cancer, which runs in my family. I'd already had several biopsies, so calling it reconstructive made it even more foolish. And while I remained sober as a recovered alcoholic, I acted like an alcoholic with food, which won't land you in a jail cell for a DUI but did land me on a doctor's table for open-heart surgery by 2019.

One wouldn't think an amicable divorce would produce PTSD, but it is considered trauma in and of itself, and many people in families suffer no matter how well they cope.

The Mayo Clinic defines PTSD symptoms as falling into four categories: intrusive memories, avoidance, negative changes in thinking and mood, and changes in physical and emotional reactions. I practiced avoidance through my food addiction, putting on weight. I became much more irritable as a person. I had lots of memories of my own childhood divorce intruding as if present-day. I experienced numbness as part of the shock and denial from the grief of losing the marriage. Yes, even if you *want* out of the marriage, you will grieve its loss. You anticipate freedom, but don't expect that divorce is an emotional prison with no escape.

An overview from Psychcentral.com offers signs of PTSD in children and adults. In your children, the signs of trauma are developmental transgression, weight changes, separation anxiety, changes in sleep patterns, nightmares, emotional outbursts, changes in academic performance, social withdrawal, and sudden changes in behavior.

In adults, signs of trauma include exhibiting symptoms of personality disorders, persistent depression and anxiety, insecure attachment styles, nightmares, emotional outbursts, regression, avoidant behavior, and isolation from loved ones.

The question is, do you really want to set yourself, your spouse, and your children up for this kind of chaos? It doesn't just affect you; it can also impact your friends and family, who have to watch everything unfold. That's called vicarious trauma.

Divorce is a story you and family members will have to keep telling the rest of your lives.

Don't Add to your Child's ACE Score

It helps when you identify as being part of a population in need of extra care and comfort. That way, you'll be more inclined to recognize your decision-making processes might be coming from a place of injury rather than freedom and bravado.

If I had had more compassion for my own history, I might have had more forgiveness for not being perfect and allowed for course correction rather than calling it quits. Part of me feels I had no tolerance for the slightest discomfort, like I had a short fuse that had been frayed a long time ago. This is a quality that grown children of divorce, unfortunately, share. Resilience is somehow missing.

In my mind, prior to divorce, a physical affair meant marriage would be over with, and when I knew I wanted to go have one, I felt it best to leave first rather than completely disgrace the marriage. But as we established earlier, it had already been adultery in the heart. But that's when I asked for a divorce, which turned out to be the ultimate disgrace in my case. In my mind then, I was trying to preserve the dignity of the marriage by walking away.

Only time and God can iron out this kind of twisted thought process.

Maybe we cheaters don't deserve sympathy, but we might garner more understanding and less toxic anger from our loved ones when they realize many of us are driven by untreated childhood wounds, even when we think we've healed many already. It's definitely more about "the past," even when the cheater is blaming the spouse for leaving. In weak cases of divorce, parents run from marital intimacy when confronted with facing their own inner work. I did, and I was already pretty good at inner work.

Hear me now: If you're cheating on your spouse, even if it's just beginning stage flirting, there's a stronger likelihood you have childhood abuse issues driving that behavior and not just some early mid-life crisis. Your straying heart has something to hide even before you create something to hide. In fact, creating an affair is the symptom you're hiding something deeper.

This brings us to a helpful tool known as your "ACE Score." This stands for Adverse Childhood Experiences. Would you like to take the test?[12] It can help you see just how many childhood factors might be influencing your adult decisions today. You can find the ACE Questionnaire for Adults at www.acesaware.org. Question #2: "Did you ever lose a parent through divorce, abandonment, death, or other reason?"

I scored 9/10 on the test, having a parent in prison being the only one I couldn't check. The ACE score showed my vulnerability to infidelity, addiction, domestic violence, and repeated divorce. It showed me that these factors are more likely causing my behavior than whatever my spouse was doing or not doing. If you already have a high ACE score, you might want to slow down and consider if these are factoring into your divorce decision without your awareness.

My high ACE score also showed me my desperate need for God's healing power in my life and for a successful marriage.

Research suggests a link between your ACE score and the increased likelihood of engaging in infidelity as an adult. Here are some of the

---

[12] www.acesaware.org, "Learn About Screening" tab, menu choice Screening Tools, test for adults.

statistics: A study published in the Journal of Marriage and Family found that 43 percent of adults who experienced parental divorce during childhood reported infidelity in their own relationships. Another study published in the Journal of Family Issues found that 55.6 percent of adults who experienced childhood trauma (including abuse and parental divorce) reported engaging in infidelity. Another study published in the Journal of Sex Research found that adults who experienced childhood abuse were more likely to engage in infidelity (34.6 percent) compared to those without a history of abuse (21.1 percent).

Do online searches about divorce regret to build your case for staying married. An article by Ann Gold Buscho, Ph.D, on divorce regrets names them: The emotional upheaval from it is far greater than expected. They underestimated the impact of the divorce on the children. The financial consequences created new hardships. Successive relationships failed. They discovered loneliness, realizing the spouse had been their best friend. They were met with stigma, rejection, and judgment from friends and family. They realized they'd been impulsive and could have worked harder to think through the outcomes.

Of those remaining 70 percent of people who divorce who don't regret it, hardly any of them with children could deny the impact on their children except if it's to save their lives. That leaves a lot of room for staying together for the children.

Prayer

Lord, show me the way to live with my marriage so that I don't choose the trauma of divorce.

Questions

1. Am I trying to escape something from my own childhood by initiating divorce?
2. Am I willing to choose anxiety as a way of life for my family?
3. Is there a spiritual alternative to dealing with my marital anxiety?
4. Is divorce "worth it?" Why?
5. Have I spoken to at least one married couple who is glad they didn't divorce?

Antidote #4

Remember the Benefits of Full-Time Parenting

"God has spoken plainly, and I have heard it many times: Power, O God, belongs to you; unfailing love, O Lord, is yours."
~ **Psalm 62:11**

According to Proverbs 12:15, *"Fools think their own way is right, but the wise listen to others."*

So, why does divorce often bring so much sadness and anxiety? Because you've cut in half the time shared between parents and children for the rest of their childhoods. That's if you share equal custody. If you have full-custody or no custody, one parent becomes a perpetual visitor, outcast, or both. That might be desirable in cases of abuse, but where there is no abuse, weak cases are full of faulty reasons for creating half-time parents.

The problem with half-time parenting is you lose sight of your children and have half the input you used to have, and no input on the other parent's parenting. You have half as much supervision for your children as you would have kept. So, for helicopter or hovering types, it's a crash landing. For avoidant parents, it spells disaster because no one's on board. For those who are neither, you'll constantly miss your children. And if you don't, it could be because you're distracted by the mess being made of your personal and professional life as a result of divorce trauma.

You can't be there to help mitigate for your children the very things you are leaving your spouse over, leaving them to navigate and fend for themselves without you. And you don't have this check system of support on yourself so your spouse can protect them from you when you falter in parenting. With this self-sufficiency in solo parenting, you sacrifice checks and balances. And you might have too much pride as a divorced parent to call the other parent if you needed such support, and they might have too much pride to call you. I found this out because we did call each other over the years as needed, but ours was a co-parenting exception. I noticed most other parents in my sphere did not have this same-page parenting experience of checks and balances.

Out of this half-timing sprouts all kinds of room for other people to enter the family scene, so be forewarned of the risks. There are certain things I learned later about divorced family dynamics that were risks I didn't consider ahead of time. For example, how can the oldest child get "spousified" and/or "parentified" after divorce? The well-meaning parents usually don't know it, but the child becomes a replacement, emotionally and mentally, taking on the absent role in *both* houses. This may take the form of decision-making, parenting the younger siblings, confiding, advice-seeking, caretaking, and adultified conversations where the parent and child are more like peers.

This unintentional covert emotional incest is hard to pinpoint and prevent. A parent might turn to the child with successive partner problems or, worse, problems with the other parent. This problem-solving creates all kinds of issues, including allegiance, loyalty, betrayal, and conflict. The child has conflicted feelings of not wanting this intimate spot in their parent's life, but not wanting to risk their rejection should they resist it. Remember, it's two losses for each child of divorce, not one. They lose both parents, not just the one who moves out. So they make every effort to hold onto both of them in emotional gymnastics we can't even imagine, which also might differ from child to child. In many cases, the word emotional *incest* is too strong, but it displaces parental and adult energy, and it creates problems for the children. Unconsciously they try to fill the space where the other parent isn't anymore.

They may become confidantes or advisors regarding the parent's new romantic exploits, which further invites resentment and sadness, but also an unfair role as the loyalty with the original parent feels betrayed. I'm appalled that I exposed my children to such risks without knowing they existed as potential dynamics, *even though it happened in my own family growing up.*

What does this do to brain development that isn't even complete until the age of 25?

When it comes to siblings, there's a whole new regime among them after divorce, and it doesn't include you. They're on their own now as the *only* part of the original family that remains together, so a lot of pressure is put on them to behave in the new family situations. They move with each other between homes, so the bond they create is one neither parent will ever have access to, ever again. It's different from the bond they created together in one home; it's a bond built on "we have to survive this together," and like it or not, it's a bond that doesn't include either parent this time. "Mom and Dad's divorce" becomes a topic here on out in their lives, coming up whenever it's needed or has intruded on some aspect of their future lives. Those are secret conversations you caused and will never be part of. No one ever talks about this secret divide that divorce creates: It's an us vs. them between the divorcing parents and the surviving children. If they get along, they forever have to navigate two homes until one parent dies.

Likewise, it's much harder to be a single parent than you might think. Now that there's only one parent, the older siblings take up the parenting in each of the homes where Mom or Dad left, and then it changes over at the next home to the other way. They just naturally fall into it; try to intervene and prevent it from happening, and you're going against the survival skills necessary to confront divorce dynamics, which force them into those roles automatically. It's not like the children want it or the parents defer. It's just the nature of divorce to destabilize everyone's role. While the eldest has to be in charge, the baby has to be good so nothing else goes wrong. The lost middle child doesn't know where to turn, and so acts out. Of course, there are variations, exceptions, and opposite turnouts, but these dynamics are examples of the impact of divorce. Once set in motion, they're very hard to outwit.

The most horrific consequences of divorce occur in the nastiest of conflicts when one parent seeks retribution by ending the children's lives to hurt the other parent. There was a time when some of these parents could never imagine such a thing ever happening between them. We think to ourselves, *how can a parent do such a thing?* Filicide, parents killing their children, is the extreme opposite of staying for the children, and it isn't divorce; it's death. In essence, their divorce kills the children. The risk for potential chaos in divorce is enormous, volatile, and unpredictable. The point here is weak cases can avert escalation into strong cases for divorce. *You cannot predict anyone's response to the trauma of divorce.* Consider yourself lucky at the moment if your case for divorce is weak; it will be that much easier to reverse.

Consider the Family Life that You Risk Losing.

It's helpful to pause and think about the things you'll never experience together as a family again, under one roof, all in the same place. This "halving" is just representative of the total experiences you lose altogether as you try to recreate traditions and family routines *by yourself.*

Think of the little things: summer vacation, day trips, family outings, going to the movies, dining out, grocery shopping, running errands, game nights, road trips, holiday traditions like picking out a Christmas tree, or even just those routine family meetings.

And when an emergency happens? If you have shared custody, you're only half as likely to be there when it counts.

Every single ride to and from school until they learn to drive.

No more birthdays together for the children or the adults as one in the same home. You'll never make a cake for your spouse in front of your children ever again.

Buying and wrapping gifts? That's all on you from now on. No more opening presents from your spouse in front of the kids. Even if you do, it won't feel the same as when you were together, and you'll start seeing it all in a new light later on.

You'll never be able to ask your spouse for help again in the same ways. For a cry in the night that needs to be heard, reassurance on your parenting interactions, reminding you of who you are, and mostly, hands-on help in raising the children together. If you think your other parent doesn't help now, just wait until complete absence occurs.

You won't get to grow old together, grandparent together, die together.

Here's a big one: you won't get to reminisce together, cultivate memories, stir each other's memories, and find ways to preserve those memories for your children. Instead, you're dividing photographs, trying to make two whole families out of one family. There are now two families that always miss one biological parent. Every time parents or grown children look back at family pictures from before the divorce, there's this wistful agony.

You might not live as long, if you divorce. Did you know married couples live longer? As we established earlier, children from intact families live, on average, five years longer than those from divorced families. Remarriage doesn't even make up for that shortfall, because of the divorce impact coming beforehand. Do you realize that you are about to shorten your life, your children's lives, and their other parent's life, by divorcing?

You won't get to cook together as a family, put the children to bed together, stay up late after they go to bed, talk about the day at work, plan your next trips, or even make your plans together. And here's a tough one: your children can never wake you up in the same bed together as a couple ever again.

If you're thinking right now, *"I really don't care,"* these are all the things you take for granted right now, and one day, divorce will make it look like you had it made.

As you go through the day today, be mindful of the life you've built, the routines you've made, the traditions you've kept, and the plans you have as a family. See if it takes on greater meaning when you suddenly think of it as *all gone.* You'll start from scratch in one home, and your children will go back to square one in both homes. It's almost as though the original family vanishes.

Weighing Loss of Full-time Access

Divorce is willing to sacrifice the children to be away from the perceived impact of the spouse. The mindset of putting the children first requires not being willing to sacrifice your full-time status as a parent, able to remain 24/7 in the lives of your children.

I did not think this through. In my mind, I wasn't losing the children at all. I felt I was gaining freedom. But the freedom I sought was from internal pain I couldn't face. By my decision to divorce, I would add to my pain in unimaginable ways, because to that point, I had not been without my children, ever.

Divorce was soon to teach me that I was losing their childhoods, the continuity of their day to day, the full story, their comprehensive experience. There are no words to put to this loss except you can't get it back once you create the scenario.

Just as the statistics show shortening of life spans, to me the underlying reasons are that the loss is so profound, it takes your breath away. It leads to suicidal parents thinking, "I don't want to live without my kids." With these thoughts, you can call the California Parent & Youth Helpline at 855-427-2736. Parents Anonymous, a non-profit, runs it.

And no one wants to acknowledge that if adults feel this way, imagine how the children feel at their vulnerable ages. To have to learn to live without your parents, alternately, over and over again, is an enormous burden on their young lives.

If wanting out is somehow at the deeper level of not wanting the full-time stresses along with those rewards of parenting, divorce has alternatives – nannies, babysitters, family members, or other parenting arrangements for your married home. Sometimes we just need a break, not a divorce.

Notice I didn't get into money issues in this book. I avoided them purposely. My parents fought over money their entire lives, until they died. While they were busy thinking money was the problem, the solution, and the only thing that mattered, I was collecting these other varied experiences and examples to share with you that I felt were more important for a book than money. It's the children we have to spare from divorce, not our bank accounts.

Your time with your children is priceless. Don't be so willing to give it away completely. Don't force the other parent of your child to give it away because you want to leave. The cost is too great for everyone. One day you'll find Club Thirty is a dead end.

Prayer

Lord, help me count the value of and the blessings in the family system as it is right now. What corrections do I need to make?

Questions

1. What does it mean to me that my time with my children will be less once we are divorced?
2. Divorce is like starting from scratch to build two new families. Have I thought about the work involved in that?
3. Make a list of all the traditions we've built and shared over the years.
4. Look over the past year of the things we've done together as a family.
5. Think of the things ahead we would still want to do as a family, especially at the significant milestones of our children's lives.

Antidote #5

Healing from Old Wounds

"For I will restore health to you and heal you of your wounds, says the Lord."
~ **Jeremiah 30:17**

Have you heard the expression, "Hurt people hurt people?" It's true. If someone is considering taking an action like divorce that hurts the entire family, it's worth taking a look at what internal pain is causing it. Even though I'd already divorced, it was important to take responsibility to find the sources of harming others in my life, to stop the trend, and to make amends.

How did I not see that leaving and hurting him was also leaving and hurting the children? My rejection of his love is also a rejection of their love for him. It doesn't support their love for him; it injures it. It hurts them to see their father suffer. It hurts him to see the children suffer. This is a bigger wound than you think. You can't separate your children from the divorce experience. They go through it with you.

The lie I told myself was: "There's something wrong with my marriage." The truth was, there was something wrong with me I didn't want to face. Divorce, in these cases, never makes sense to the children. They can't see what you're leaving the other parent for, so it's bewildering to them, making them doubt their love and question it, as well as doubt and question the love that comes from future partners. Mindset: "If this can break up, anything can."

It Wasn't About Him

I wish someone had flat-out told me that my desire to leave my spouse wasn't about him or the marriage. In case you need to hear it, I'll tell you: Your urge to leave your spouse *might not be about your spouse.*

In my case, it was about running from these childhood demons and also a consequence of the emotional infidelity. Both create a self-absorption that makes a mother emotionally unavailable, though she may be going through all the motions of caretaking and caregiving. I also didn't know that my so-called "safe" one-way emotional affairs were taking me emotionally and mentally away from my children, not just my husband.

I had to learn to connect in a deeper way to my children after the divorce to fill in the vacancies. Parental selfishness is a barrier to children. I wish I had cleared away the blockage interfering with my empathy for the children much, much earlier, so I could have considered what divorce would do to them.

This meant facing the damage from adultery in the heart, and the impact of running from incest memories rather than staying within the marriage to face them. This is the personal work anyone who remains in marriage long enough has to confront – anything from the past that comes up to be healed.

I've come to believe that if something doesn't heal within the marriage, it weakens and then can break the marriage. And if the marriage breaks, it's that much harder to get to the healing that was avoided, because divorce trauma compounds the original injury rather than allowing for its healing. You'll have to heal from divorce now as well as the original causes.

And you'll never get to know what family life would have been like had you stayed, or how the children would have been influenced otherwise. You only have divorce as the influence to blame for everything that occurs from then on in family life. You're signing up for a lifetime of wistful thinking, and everything that happens gets compared to an alternate script that doesn't exist. It's also distracting to evaluate everything that goes on with the children as the fault of parents divorcing, especially when they face challenges. So, the inordinate guilt is a constant nag, as is the burden of blame your spouse was predisposed to feel toward you as a result of leaving.

Deeper Reasons

There were reasons I was hell-bent on divorce than could ever be checked on a court form. They were far deeper than I ever imagined and had nothing to do with the children's father or the marriage. This was hard to discover once I was a Christian. There was a lot of healing to do.

The date of filing for divorce caught my attention as a red flag. Only after my divorce did I pose the question, why do I make such radical spontaneous decisions every early April? As you know from my story, abuse in the past was a catalyst for wrong responses. Had I looked at the springtime antics each year from my diary, I could see "early April" spelled out lifetime landmines in my intimate relationships. I would quit a job, start a business, break up with boyfriends, get engaged, then add to the list in 2008, get divorced. A common denominator, of course, was a manic spell, living with the condition of bipolar disorder, but *why* the manic spell every April, and even on meds?

I traced back April dates in my history. I looked up a 1985 calendar. Sure enough, it was April 5, 1985, when I experienced rape at a college fraternity house. It made more sense now why, in 2008, I would file for divorce on April 4. All the pieces fell into place with the impulsive, radical early April changes. Back to the theory about shifting circumstances to circumvent truth.

When there's abuse in the past, it can recreate abuse in the present – in essence, a traumatic stress response of recreating harm. Simply put, acting out is really an attempt to get it out of your system, but all it does is reinforce the trauma. Unpacked, it just perpetuates harm. Hurt people hurt people.

The corrective action for this one is to *wait it out*. The urge to file may have passed. Had I made the association between past trauma and current behavior, I believe I could have stopped in my tracks. If I had just made it past that annual splitting-off behavior, I might not have taken action. I didn't put it together until far too late that the timing was suspect.

Another math problem I solved way too late is this: My mother was also 43 with three children when she divorced! Lights flashing "Repeat Warning Ahead," couldn't someone have warned me that the biological urge to repeat history was upon me? Maybe I could have written the prophetic date on the calendar. If anything, in therapy, I could have become conscious of the underlying vulnerability simply based on the template I was given. This could have clued me in that I had certain obligations to wait out the unconscious blueprints within. If I could just make it past the more vulnerable phases of being married with children, I might have come out stronger for it and not threatened the family system. Instead, it broke, like clockwork, according to the previous schedule imposed.

I'm not blaming my mother for my decision, as if victim to a default mode; I just wish I'd been aware of the repetitive nature of the divorce legacy in spite of my noblest intentions and premarital efforts to overcome it. I was not immune to it, no matter how much I prided myself on overcoming it to that point by remaining faithfully married for 15 years. It was always going to be a looming threat, and I could have accepted it as such.

The ages of my daughters at the time most definitely helped the unconscious memories of my father's abuse to surface. Not only was the one daughter 7 when I chose to divorce – that's the age my parents divorced – but having a baby produced its own vulnerabilities. I had come off medications under supervision by the Women's Life Center at UCLA during the pregnancy,[13] so I wish now I had ridden out the desire to create further instability. Although I returned to medications during the third trimester of

---

[13] Women's Life Center. A clinic of the Semel Institute for Neuroscience and Human Behavior, David Geffen School of Medicine, University of California Los Angeles.

pregnancy, I should have given myself the gift of time. I didn't connect my drive to divorce to instability.

Best intentions aside, when you divorce, the reality is that the past gets repeated in one way or another. There were many patterns I set in motion by divorcing that I see now that God could have healed in advance of it, had I called upon Him. Not only did I have to work toward forgiveness of my father, but I had to forgive myself for acting out in response to it, in my marriage. I also had to seek forgiveness from my spouse for the cheating.

I chose to come out publicly in a book over incest because there are too many women having affairs out there because their fathers got to them first. How does childhood incest lead to marital cheating? For me, it was an attempt to take ownership and control back over sexuality unfairly claimed by the father. But cheating on one's spouse then further disowns the experience, driving it deeper into the mire, burying it all over again in a mass array of false affections projected onto other men.

Divorce was far less about him and the marriage than I ever thought. It was all about me, and that selfishness was the root problem. Unfortunately, that meant I wasn't thinking about others and the profound impact divorce would have on everyone.

Check your personal historical facts; they may stop you in your tracks. We know we are all seeking freedom. But are you running from the marriage, or are you running from yourself?

While writing this book I discovered another injustice in unconscious timing. Every January I still grieve for the miscarried baby from 2000 – January 25 that year. It was January 23 in 2008 when I officially announced in a counseling session that I wanted a divorce. Did you know most people separate or ask for divorce in January?[14] Post-*holiday* stress disorder! January would have also been the month to abstain from divorce rather than bury and avert my past.

The bottom line on calendar dates is don't let your traumas unconsciously create more trauma.

Origins of Selfishness

Still not convinced that divorce isn't the right choice? Let me walk you through a different scenario. You may be suffering from the "My case is different" defense mechanism I didn't know

---

[14] Newsweek, Jan. 10, 2024, "Here's Why January is the Most Popular Month for Divorce," Suzanne Blake.

was operating. Give it a rest, just for now. You can see the alternate script to your current married life without having to ruin your marriage, just by continuing to read on.

Divorce is a huge responsibility you're taking on, and it has far-reaching implications for the grandchildren you don't even have yet. If not repeated generationally, it's an entire legacy you'll create and hand down. And everyone has to live within its governing dynamics for the rest of their lives.

I cringe still at how my selfishness put me before the breaking hearts of my children and their father. I wanted out no matter the cost, and that was it. No more negotiation, no more discussion, no more counseling. Their words from back then only impacted me years later at the feeling level, revealing the absence of my attunement to them at the time. I believe they've forgiven me, but that isn't the point; I needed this fine attunement at the time it mattered most.

There is a difference between guarding one's heart in its selfishness and guarding one's heart to protect it from selfishness. I see now that, at the time, there was no room in the vacancy of my heart space for the consideration of other people's feelings. Find the nearest person to you to read this to you aloud: *"Your children will never see you and their parents again in the same home as a unit."* If you have no emotional response to this, chances are you're shut down.

And if you're in the middle of an affair, you may be buzzing with energy now on fire like a teen-ager on first love because you're driven like I was, thinking some better life is out there waiting for you, when really all that's waiting for you is a type of crash and burn you haven't experienced yet. If you think marital strife is exhausting now, wait until you discover the drain that divorce puts on the relationship dynamics.

As a child, my home life felt like it drained the life out of me. And if a reservoir of energy started to accumulate, my father, mother, or stepmother would notice, and like emotional vampires, who always know when to strike, they would suck the energy right out of my soul.

Chronically sick with colds, mostly sore throats, I could get my mother to stay home with me. She was a compulsive shopper and manic spender. I hated shopping at Saks Fifth Avenue and I.Magnin, but I knew going along with her was the way to feel her presence hours on end, even though it ended in a dreadful malaise. I felt spoiled and rotten, hiding her shoe count from my inquiring father, eager to nail her in court.

The constant mental task afflicting me: Who was telling the truth, which parent was lying, who was right? One of them was the bad guy, but they each said it was the other, so it was up to me to figure out. I'd become a lawyer, go to Harvard, and promised Mom I'd have Dad locked up for not sending the child support checks he said went to her shoes. Was that true? Didn't she spend it on us? Our insides would freeze when Dad would ask what Mom got us for Christmas. There was no right answer, so it didn't matter to lie. We would just make up stories and hope they were true.

One day, Dad swore to us, the children, in a letter that he never lied to us. That was a lie right there. We have no idea what prompted such a confession. One summer vacation, he told us we were in a different city, so when we talked to our mother, she wouldn't know where we were to track us down. And when my travel diary disappeared after our trip to Europe, Mom said it would end up in court because I put so many details into our trip, so then it was my fault she'd lose something. *Would Dad really steal my diary?*

The interrogations on both ends were torture, both in the dread of anticipation, the shame of the grilling session, and the fear of the outcomes in the aftermath of what was disclosed. No matter what I said, it was wrong.

This is just one page describing the mental strain of divorce. Those of us who have already come from divorce have no idea of the revisitation that occurs of the past pain. You'll relive your own childhood divorce all over again at new and different levels. Just about the time you maybe almost got over it as an adult, you go in for another round.

Until years after divorce, I didn't see my situation in any Scriptural references to divorce in the Bible. I saw my case was meant for staying, because he had become a believer in high school. The fault here was not consulting any religious text for guidance. The Bible makes concessions for divorce. I didn't fit any one of them. Do you? Look it up now while you're still married. I didn't look up these Scriptures until way too late to do any good. I also didn't avail myself of any religious help, a profound regret.

For example, 1 Corinthians 7:12-16 says: "***12** Now, I will speak to the rest of you, though I do not have a direct command from the Lord. If a fellow believer has a wife who is not a believer and she is willing to continue living with him, he must not leave her. **13** And if a believing woman has a husband who is not a believer and he is willing to continue living with her, she must not leave him. **14** For the believing wife brings holiness to her marriage, and the believing husband brings holiness to his marriage. Otherwise, your children would not be holy, but now they are holy. **15** (But if the husband or wife who isn't a believer insists on leaving, let them go.*

In such cases the believing husband or wife is no longer bound to the other, for God has called you to live in peace.) **16** *Don't you wives realize that your husbands might be saved because of you? And don't you husbands realize that your wives might be saved because of you?"*

When I read this passage, I realized I didn't fit these other situations either. I had a faithful spouse, in fact, he had grounds to divorce me, but didn't. I had no reason to divorce him.

Take Matthew 19:9, where Jesus says, **"***And I tell you this, whoever divorces his wife and marries someone else commits adultery—unless his wife has been unfaithful."*

I didn't have any reason, infidelity or abandonment. In 1 Corinthians 7:15, Paul explains another situation: *"But if the husband or wife who isn't a believer insists on leaving, let them go. In such cases the believing husband or wife is no longer bound to the other, for God has called you to live in peace."*

I didn't fit this scenario either. So what exactly are illegitimate reasons for divorce? You'd need to ask a pastor for a complete answer. But I knew this much: there was no domestic violence or active addiction in my home to point to as a cause.

As explained in the first chapter, my reasons for wanting a divorce weren't about him at all. If your spouse is behaving well, it's all the more likely your reasons for wanting a divorce are buried deep in your heart, not his or her actions. If you can't point to anything wrong with them, you're lucky. If you *can* point to what's wrong, it gives you excuses to leave that aren't the real reasons. If you keep saying, "It's not about you; it's me who's changed," then keep changing; you're not done. Yes, it's about you, but for the wrong reasons: it's selfishness, not self-preservation or self-care.

Legal reasons for divorce didn't apply to me either. Though I checked "irreconcilable differences" as the reason for petitioning divorce, this wasn't true, as it's described in more detail on the actual form as "irretrievably broken and the spouses cannot reconcile." It's not fair; one person may desperately want it to work out. I look back now and see that I forced his hand to sign the papers just by insisting on divorce. Like I said, call it "no-fault" divorce in California all you want; it just means your reasoning doesn't have to be legitimate. It's always someone's fault. We tell the children they aren't at fault, blame the other spouse, and have no clue where we're really at fault as the petitioner. *Divorce is so ugly, no one wants to look at it in the mirror.*

There was no abuse and nothing life-threatening going on. There was literally nothing to warrant divorcing him, and he even said so himself. There was way more hope for change to occur in my thinking than I ever thought at the time. In just six months, after 16 years, for no good reason, the marriage was over.

For all the time spent married, I could have tried harder. But since my exit plan was about getting away from myself, now I can see how I was willing to sacrifice the marriage to escape. The irony is, that he lost me, but I couldn't lose me. I didn't realize that if I divorced, it all would follow me, and the very same issues would now further fragment our even more depleted family support system.

Luckily, I've done all my advanced thinking *now,* proving it's never too late to get the right mindset. You might not have a husband anymore, but you'll recover your lost mind, fill your empty heart, and Jesus can mend your shredded soul.

A Glimpse of Hope

Let's say you're married right now, and you still feel like two people, not one flesh. Just think of the growth possibilities to learn to become one together. You don't have to divorce to become whole; you can discover how to embody "the one" by staying married. Instead of going two separate ways because you feel like two, take a step forward to become one for the first time. It's an experience you haven't had yet. Me neither!

It's too late for those of us who regret our divorces, but it's not too late for you. If you haven't stepped into the divorce arena yet, you perhaps have guilt just thinking about divorce. Good! It means you have a conviction that it's the wrong thing to do. That's what guilt is for: To keep you on the right path before you take actions you'll regret later. So consider it evidence that your conscience is looking out for you.

I'm not sure why I didn't feel guilty before or during the divorce. It only hit me afterward. Maybe it was because I thought I was doing the right thing. Turns out if you don't have a conviction, you won't feel guilt, like a remorseless killer. I lacked conviction divorce was wrong for me. I didn't even think divorce was wrong for my parents. I just thought the way they went about it was wrong by fighting so much. I was ignorant.

How do you get a spiritual conviction if you don't have it? That's a good question. Spending time with the Lord in Bible Scripture is one way to achieve it, but what if you don't know Jesus or aren't religious? Think about your wedding vows. Did you not mean them?

Here's what conviction sounds like: "I can't do this to my children. It would hurt them." And,

"I have to honor my wedding vows. I made a commitment to this marriage."

I lacked those feelings and thoughts. Do you lack them, too? Read on.

Over time, I regretted it more and more, not less and less. That's because the full weight of my burden cast onto the family didn't show itself until much farther along in my spiritual growth. As I grew in my faith, I faced the Godly sorrow required of anybody who must answer to God about their past behaviors.

The Lord indicated to me through these painful feelings that a book to help others would be a good way to redeem myself.

How do I know this? Self-interest is a marriage killer, because enduring marriages are based on sacrifice, not selfishness. "I want out" wasn't reason enough! What does it mean to stay for the children? I didn't explore that option long enough. I should have stayed just for the children if I couldn't find other reasons. Children are the only reason a couple with children need to remain married. It is the best reason of all to remain married, when you have children.

Putting Children First

"Children are a gift from the Lord; they are a reward from Him."
~ **(Psalms 127:3)**

The hardest lesson I've learned comes from my own story. I think if I took time to tell myself, *"Do not make your husband (and, as a result, your children) pay for what your father does to you, past and present."* (If a man, the reverse would be true for your wife). Things would have been different. If any of you need to hear those words, you just did from me. No therapist treated me to this insight at the time. I never sought out church pastors or religious counseling of any kind. The Lord revealed it to me years later, when I finally did develop the kind of relationship with Jesus that I wished I'd had when I needed it married.

Because children are God's reward, they deserve to be prized! I see in retrospect that it's ok to not take the temperature of the marriage for once, and focus on what is best for the children, only. As a couple, we might have survived that early childhood rearing phase if I had just forgotten about myself for a moment and hadn't made the marriage the problem. My spouse implored me to wait, and I wouldn't listen. We could have spent the remainder of our lives dealing with our own issues.

Because children are a reward, my obligation as a married mother would be to put their happiness before mine. It puzzles me why, after the divorce, I had no trouble putting them first before the relationships that came along, but somehow was not able to put them first when it came to the most important relationship of all – with their father. It still puzzles me why I had it backward, even though I've poured out all my conscious reasoning here.

There's a misconception that if you put the children first, your marriage will suffer. But I believe putting the children first really honors the marriage and makes it endure. It's true that time itself changes things. Ask any couple that waited it out.

She will never see you both together in one home! Haunting words that replay in my heart.

The simple wisdom asked and uttered from the humble hearts of our children, past, present, and future, is truly astonishing, admonishing, and corrective. They can be our toughest critics, can't they? When they question our decisions, even at young ages, it's seen as disrespectful or questioning authority. But they're right, and they have the words, and their questions are often so profound we scramble to give them answers we don't have because we haven't asked ourselves those same questions yet.

I wished I had valued them so much that I would never break apart the family, never take their father from them, and never take myself away from them like I did. I've heard parents say, "I could never do that to my children," and I'm envious of their conviction. I didn't have it. It just wasn't there.

No matter what you tell your children, they'll still naturally find a way to blame themselves for your troubles. *If you love me, why can't you stay together? What did I do wrong? Is this because I don't do what I'm told? I promise I'll be better. Does Mom/Dad not love me anymore – is that why they want to leave?* Your actions speak louder than your words, and you cannot control what they hear or think in response to your actions. They might start wondering about their role in your divorce, which can lead to feelings of depression. They become withdrawn, anxious, and find it hard to communicate with other children.

When I say divorce is the loss that keeps losing, one aspect involves the constant reminders of it for the rest of your life: Every time you leave the house to go to the other parent's house to get your children. Every time they tell you as adults, they're busy with Mom/Dad. Every time there's an outing, vacation, or celebration without you. Every time you don't learn about news or developments first. Every time you give a child's address on forms. Every time someone asks you if you're married, divorced, or single, on intake forms or applications. The final date may be stamped on a divorce decree, but the story will reverberate and follow you for the rest of your life.

> *"Now my soul is deeply troubled. Should I pray, 'Father, save me from this hour'? But this is the very reason I came!"*
>
> ~ **(John 12:27)**

To this day, I cannot comprehend how I could divorce as a mother given what a negative impact divorce had upon me growing up, and how hard I worked at being able to get married in the first place because of childhood divorce. This is the biggest sense of failure – that even trying my best, I still didn't spare my own children. Instead, I hurt my children with the very thing that hurt me the most.

It will be up to the three daughters to break the chain on this legacy. The best I could do is pass on lessons to persevere with marriage, not by example but by what I call "the negative template." It's quite possible that their own experience of divorce growing up would double their commitment to stay married to not pass on the legacy. I just wish I could have broken the chain for them. Now, they're tasked with being chain-breakers on the legacy of divorce.

Ask yourself: Do I want to undermine their future relationship commitments given how the divorce trauma is something they'll have to work at, face those issues with like a burden or a curse? They have to deal with its impact. So, do I want to saddle my children with their own divorce story?

So it isn't so much "passing on divorce" that is the regret, but passing on the divorce wound – the hurt. Divorce hurt me, and at a vulnerable point in my marriage, I turned around and hurt them. They had to heal from the divorce wound, too, and unwillingly joined the other club known as Children of Divorce.

Their wound has many layers: Children have to watch the parent left behind suffer a broken heart. Being hurt about that parent leaving even when the other parent is the one who filed for divorce. It hurts that parents can't put their issues aside long enough to protect their children from such hurt. Hurt all around in the selfishness implicit in divorcing, to begin with, which then leads to feelings of being unloved. It's a much deeper well than anyone headed that way ever stops to think about, which is why Club Thirty's percentage is so high.

I believe my own pain prevented me from anticipating theirs. But you don't know you're in pain when you're in any kind of addictive mode.

As a parent, repression makes you 1) clueless and 2) unavailable to others.

Your Children's Entire World Depends Upon You Two.

I secretly hoped that my parents would get back together, and that my Dad would come home. One day, he just never came back home after that last business trip. Then we only saw him during the summers and Christmas because he moved to the opposite side of the country. I'd burn with envy over happy-ending movies like "The Parent Trap." Wanting my parents together seemed like a dream too good to dream, leaving me feeling like an outcast of the kingdom. My life always felt 10 degrees off-center.

I longed for my Dad ever since he left home, and it felt like he left me for another woman when he remarried. He preferred her over my own mother and me. Later he said he was just leaving our mother and "not leaving us," but it felt like a rejection of all of us.

As a child, I felt hopeless, helpless and hateful. I kept waiting for the episode of "The Brady Bunch" to address something about divorce, but they never did explain why Carol and Mike weren't with their former spouses anymore – although one episode suggested Mike's former wife died. Whatever happened to Carol's former husband was too shameful for TV. Alcoholic, maybe?

The desire for the two parents was there, but it was never fulfilled. In a sense, I passed on my unfulfillment by divorcing. I would have embraced wholeness by staying. I failed to recognize the deepest desire of my children to have their parents stay together. I didn't realize the impact on any of us and didn't make the connection in time.

How did this fulfillment eventually happen for me just through Jesus? The only way to describe it is that He filled in the spaces of the brokenness. He took up residence in my broken heart. He fulfilled the unfulfillment. He cured the longing, the aching desire in my heart for something I didn't even dare dream would happen – that they would get back together. He put me back together without them.

It's the substitution nature of the work at the cross that takes whatever piece is missing or broken in you, and takes the place of it. That's how Christ heals, makes complete, restores, and renews. *My parents didn't need to get back together* because I was back together in Christ. *I didn't need to get back with my former spouse* because I was put back together in Christ. Jesus does for us what no human can do. And He fills in all vacancies in the heart, because that's the nature of His love – perfect, whole, and complete. It's remarkable.

If you suffer from sabotage streaks like I did, they are unnecessary; you don't need to break apart your marriage when Christ already took the fall for not only any transgressions in your marriage, but the sins of your parents who may have abused you as well. So stop punishing yourself for all of it. Like my Jewish friend tells me, "Get off the cross; we need the wood." At the time, I didn't see divorce as sabotaging, but I sure do now.

They say we'll experience this completeness in heaven, but the real secret to life is that it's just as accessible on earth to those who are open to receiving it now. It may take a calamity like a divorce to get you there, but hopefully, whatever brokenness led to wanting a divorce is enough to invoke His healing process without destroying the family first. If we don't reach out for Christ, we're cornered by Him. That's the nature of His undying, relentless love for us.

Meanwhile, divorce is a complete joy killer. If you're unhappy now, you're thinking divorce will make you happy? There's a reason we don't wish people a happy divorce. The two don't mix. You can survive and move on, but true joy is in Him. And I can have Him in my marriage, or I can encounter Him in the pain I discover as a result of being out of my marriage. But the answer is the same, so it *isn't necessary to divorce* to find the true happiness we are talking about. End result: You'll preserve the happiness of your children's childhoods.

A Word To Those Who Regret Divorce

For people who regret divorce, no matter how long ago it was, I'm hoping you can join in the effort to prevent others from making the same mistake. The problem isn't that we regret divorce and still need to get over it; it's that we divorced in the first place. So if we can help others avoid the same pitfalls, it gives a certain redemption to the malady of remorse, don't you agree?

The cure for regret is to shift into gratitude for the marriage and the relationship it was that bore the children. But it can be quite painful to recall the good times, which is why it's easier to stay remorseful. No one wants to recall what they lost, what they gave up, and the harm they caused. Acknowledging what you left behind can intensify the guilt. Also, it tends to anger the children: "Well, then why did you leave in the first place?" It's too late to make a difference to anyone but you. But you are the person that needs this acknowledgment, because regret torments us without a purpose for good use.

Once the lesson is shared, the appreciation is what helps us move on.

I'll share my gratitude briefly, to give you an idea.

I do have the satisfaction of our daughters being born within wedlock; they were part of the sacred bond from the start. We had them 10 years after we met, so we worked out as much of our childhood issues as possible. The third child was even our final great attempt to make the marriage work, knowing we did well when it came to raising our children. So we both thought one more might convince me to stay. The marriage counselor shook her head at us. I was back to the divorce mindset after she was born. She was our "A" for effort, the ultimate gift arising from our divorce discussions.

I appreciate now what some people refer to as the endless conversation that marriage is. It never stops and can go on at any hour of the day. Particularly humorous were the middle-of-the-night laughs at our interpretations of the world and its complicated human interactions. I miss those.

Also, no matter what was going on in life, whenever I would hear his voice on the phone, all would suddenly be comforted.

I took for granted the value of having a partner to do everything with in life. And I especially took that for granted after the children were born, thinking I would do better on my own, which doesn't make sense to me now.

Who will remember that the Lord's Prayer instrumental from Paul Horn's Peace Album preceded our wedding march by Virgil Fox, or that Suzanne Ciani's instrumental "The Velocity of Love" came before that? And Enya's "Book of Days" was the song playing as we walked down the aisle after saying "I do"? Only recently did I look up the lyrics to that last song; poor choice with the last line being "This day ends together, far and away."

Ask anyone who was at our outdoor ranch wedding: Two hawks circled above and a feather fell to the pond below. These are the sacred details you want to recall before you divorce. And don't give away your wedding gown, especially if you have three daughters. Mine was only $79 in 1992 from The Horsey Place in Indio, California, a white Western style dress. I instantly regretted giving it away the moment my daughter asked if I still had it – another example of the loss that keeps losing. He has the original wedding rings because they belonged to his parents, but what did I do with the diamond engagement ring I kept? It's nowhere.

That's about all I can go into before it starts becoming idealized, insincere, or too painful for me. But you get the idea. Think about what was good about it. And all you have to do is look into the eyes of your children to know what is best about it. Can we all agree? We would not have these children if it weren't for the one person we left behind. Can we be so grateful for these children that we dare not leave their other parent?

We can find solace knowing that no matter how much pain we caused our spouse by leaving them, we gave them something that no one else could give them —the greatest joy of their lives embodied by the children. Their very existence outweighs everything. They are the summation of that marriage, not defined by divorce.

A Final Word to Married Parents

Hopefully, by realizing your children come from the marriage, you can see that you and your spouse hold a connection with the children that will always be there. So you can make it work together, or you can work around not being together. But no one else will ever hold a candle to your children's other parent in that regard – they are your children's other parent. I wish I had revered this bond before filing for divorce.

At least it wasn't too late to back up and think the correct ways about marriage, because my gratitude and honor reflects in everything I am today, apart. But it just would have been nice to figure these things out earlier.

Healing takes time, and forgiveness is key. Out of the blue 16 years after the divorce, my oldest daughter forgave me for leaving her father. I had formally asked for forgiveness four years before. Think about the magnitude of carrying that burden from the age of 10. People do not get over divorce in a few years, even five. And some parents aren't so lucky to ever be forgiven in a child's lifetime. I forgave both my parents for their divorce madness in my late 20s. But once I repeated the divorce legacy, I went through another round of hatred and blame for them. So, another round of forgiveness was required that I dealt with just between me and God. It's a lifetime of work, this loss that keeps losing. Divorce is the legacy you leave behind after you spend your entire life reckoning with it. Sparing children from divorce is worth all the effort it takes to not give up.

The illusion that your life will be the same, just minus a spouse, is not the reality. Everything in your life will change. Everything. This is what people mean when they say, "think it through." I don't know any couples who stayed married who said they should have divorced at the times they ever wanted to. They were glad they stuck it out in the long haul. Your time to stick it out is now.

Two Words to Respondents

Don't sign.

Prayer

Lord, give us a heart to hear our children and a mind to do what's right for them. Guard our hearts so that we may honor You for the sake of our children. Help us spare our children from divorce.

Final Questions

- What are my beliefs about what divorce will do for me?

- Why the rush to divorce? What could I be running to or running from?

- Do I understand what divorce will do to family life as I know it now?

- Do I think of my children enough?

- Have I thought about my children's feelings as part of my decision-making?

- Why do I want to divorce?

- Is there any behavior I'm currently doing that is bad for my marriage?

- Do I identify with the "one flesh," or do I feel like two people?
- Is there anything I need to tell my spouse in front of a counselor or pastor?
- How do my children view our marriage?
- Compared to what I tell people, what is the real reason I want to divorce?
- What are my grounds for divorce?
- Did my own ACE score reveal anything about how I'm currently viewing marriage?
- Is there anything I could be wrong about in my assessment of my marriage, my spouse, or myself?
- Is there anything going on in my life right now that is influencing my decision-making?

Epilogue

"May God give you more and more grace and peace as you grow in your knowledge of God and Jesus our Lord."
~ **2 Peter 1:2**

I do trust that by now, you're fortified by the Scripture and that the Lord has taken up the slack where you held the reigns too tightly before. My job is done. I have said the things I wish I'd been told. A special reminder to those who already regret divorcing: Attend my fellowship on Zoom[15] to help married parents on the brink of divorce. Let's talk them off the cliff together, if they, too, are suffering from a potential escapist divorce. I pray that the Lord transforms any guilt and regret you carry into lessons to help others stay married.

To the married parents: You're at the juncture. Do you proceed with divorce at all costs, or do you trust that Jesus has a different story to tell for your family life? If the Lord so guides you, please go live the original family life I wish I'd kept.

Likewise, through the course of this book, the Lord may have impressed upon your heart to seek help, make changes, and undo the harm

---

[15] On Sundays at 1 p.m. Pacific Time in the USA, Club Thirty members meet on Zoom to share lessons with married parents and pray for them. Email soulcustody.pamela@gmail.com

done. If you changed your mind and no longer want to divorce, you now have a powerful story to tell other parents who want to divorce. Tell them how you considered it and why you changed your mind. Make it a personal one-on-one ministry of your own to help other couples avoid the unnecessary divorces.

Allow the Holy Spirit to repair any damage to your marriage from your contemplation stages. Push forward with fortitude down the road to greater longevity and union. When you next hug your spouse, claim your renewed position. When you next hug your children, remember how much they value you both as their parents. Look at yourselves as a couple, like the children see you. Your role is vital. Place your family in the care of Jesus from here on out.

May the Holy Spirit continue to breathe new life into your family, day by day.

Again an encouragement from 2 Corinthians 12:9, "*My grace is all you need. My power works best in weakness.*"

Appendix

Citations

1. *Club 30 is my name rounding off the percentage who regret divorce from Page 37 of a 2016 Relationship, Marriage and Divorce survey by Avvo.com.*

2. A "rainbow" child is a term used for the child born after one was lost.

3. Food addiction recovery can be found at www.faacanhelp.org

4. Silent Auction of the oil portrait to the highest bidder. Email soulcustody.pamela@gmail.com

5. Study by D.A. Harmer et al, Journal of Psychiatric Research, 2009.

6. In California, for example, get divorce case dismissal forms at https://www.courts.ca.gov/forms.htm and search forms CIV 110 and 120.

7. www.churchinitiative.org that created DivorceCare has a marital crisis intervention tool, "Choosing Wisely." I started offering it to married couples through Pathway Church in Redlands, CA, in 2025.

8. Find more figures at momlovesbest.com, where Beth McCallum compiled 25 Children of Divorce Statistics & Facts, Feb. 18, 2025.

9. Pew Research Center, 2014.

10. www.beforeyoudivorce.org, "Choosing Wisely," a marriage crisis intervention tool in five sessions for use in church settings. Videos and workbook intended for a facilitator to work with one couple.

11. The Longevity Project, Howard Friedman, Ph.D, and Leslie R. Martin, Ph.D, 2012.

12. www.acesaware.org, "Learn About Screening" tab, menu choice Screening Tools, test for adults.

13. Women's Life Center. A clinic of the Semel Institute for Neuroscience and Human Behavior, David Geffen School of Medicine, University of California Los Angeles.

14. Newsweek, Jan. 10, 2024, "Here's Why January is the Most Popular Month for Divorce," Suzanne Blake.

15. On Sundays at 1 p.m. Pacific Time in the USA, Club Thirty members meet on Zoom to share lessons and pray for married parents who attend. Email soulcustody.pamela@gmail.com

Quiz

Are You Heading Toward Divorce Regret?

1. Does your spouse appear to be the problem? "If he/she____then I would stay married."
2. Do you think you'd be a better parent unmarried?
3. Are you currently in an extramarital affair, emotional or physical?
4. Are you wanting to divorce to be with someone else?
5. Do you know enough about commitment to marriage?
6. Have you experienced salvation in Jesus Christ?
7. Has anyone counseled or ministered to you as a couple yet?
8. Have you asked God for help with your marriage?
9. Do you think divorce will relieve your frustrations and conflicts?
10. Have you left other relationships before?

Answer key to Club Thirty: *One matching answer makes room for grace.*

1. YES
2. YES
3. YES
4. YES
5. YES
6. NO
7. NO
8. NO
9. YES
10. YES

Study Guide

1. What is your story leading up to wanting a divorce?
2. Can you trace a "Point of Return" where you first "went wrong" in your marriage?
3. Who do you turn to for advice, support, and guidance?
4. What would it take for you to change your mind about divorce?
5. Do you lean on God enough?
6. Am I in a hurry to divorce? If so, why?
7. Have I considered the emotional impact of divorce on our children?

8. Divorce isn't an event; it's a process and a long-lasting trauma. Am I prepared to consciously choose this route?

9. Look closely at any doubts I have about divorce. They may have hidden lessons for me.

10. Think about what our children have said or asked about our marriage. Sometimes, God speaks through our children. Am I really listening?

11. Is there anything I'm looking for my spouse to provide that only God can provide?

12. Is there anything I need to admit to my spouse?

13. Do I have any prior commitments or contracts made verbally or otherwise with any other person other than my spouse?

14. Has my counseling included religious discussion on the meaning and commitment of marriage?

15. Have I prayed with my spouse about our marriage?

16. Am I trying to escape something from my own childhood by initiating divorce?

17. Am I willing to choose anxiety as a way of life for my family?

18. Is there a spiritual alternative to dealing with my marital anxiety?

19. Is divorce "worth it?" Why?

20. Have I spoken to at least one married couple who is glad they didn't divorce?
21. What does it mean to me that my time with my children will be less once we are divorced?
22. Divorce is like starting from scratch to build two new families. Have I thought about the work involved in that?
23. Make a list of all the traditions we've built and shared over the years.
24. Look over the past year of the things we've done together as a family.
25. Think of the things ahead I would still want to do as a family, especially at the significant milestones of our children's lives.
26. What are my beliefs about what divorce will do for me?
27. Why the rush to divorce? What could I be running to or running from?
28. Do I understand what divorce will do to family life as I know it now?
29. Do I think of my children enough?
30. Have I thought about my children's feelings as part of my decision-making?
31. Why do I want to divorce?
32. Is there any behavior I'm currently doing that is bad for my marriage?

33. Do I identify with the "one flesh," or do I feel like two people?
34. Is there anything I need to tell my spouse in front of a counselor or pastor?
35. How do my children view our marriage?
36. Compared to what I tell people, what is the real reason I want to divorce?
37. What are my grounds for divorce?
38. Did my own ACE score reveal anything about how I'm currently viewing marriage?
39. Is there anything I could be wrong about in my assessment of my marriage, my spouse, or myself?
40. Is there anything going on in my life right now that is influencing my decision-making?

JOURNAL

JOURNAL

JOURNAL

JOURNAL

JOURNAL

JOURNAL

JOURNAL

JOURNAL

JOURNAL

JOURNAL

JOURNAL

JOURNAL

JOURNAL

JOURNAL

JOURNAL

JOURNAL

JOURNAL

JOURNAL

JOURNAL

JOURNAL

JOURNAL

www.ingramcontent.com/pod-product-compliance
Lightning Source LLC
Chambersburg PA
CBHW030438010526
44118CB00011B/696